The
Shaman
in the
Disco
and Other Dreams of
Masculinity

The Shaman in the Disco and Other Dreams of Masculinity

Men, Isolation, and Intimacy

James William Thomas, Ph.D.

iUniverse, Inc.

New York Lincoln Shanghai

The Shaman in the Disco and Other Dreams of Masculinity
Men, Isolation, and Intimacy

iUniverse books may be ordered through booksellers or by contacting:

iUniverse
2021 Pine Lake Road, Suite 100
Lincoln, NE 68512
www.iuniverse.com
1-800-Authors (1-800-288-4677)

ISBN-13: 978-0-595-40189-5 (pbk)
ISBN-13: 978-0-595-84566-8 (ebk)
ISBN-10: 0-595-40189-9 (pbk)
ISBN-10: 0-595-84566-5 (ebk)

Printed in the United States of America

In gratitude to Patricia Poggi, who, as a gifted and committed therapist, guided me on my inner journey living and writing this book, and became the shaman for me in my disco of distractions. To my dear father, Douglas Milton Thomas, for his many sacrifices for his family, and for his passionate enthusiasm for life—gone from this world to where?—but you are always here in my heart, Dad, where we finally learned to share life. And to my best friend and wonderful wife, Pam, who has always supported this book through thick and thin, and who is a rare beacon of life in this rich, shimmering darklight. I am grateful we are together. And to everyone out there searching for love, who like me, need reminding that it begins with loving ourselves.

In fact it seems to me as if the alienation which so long separated me from the world has become transferred into my own inner world, and has revealed to me an unexpected unfamiliarity with myself.

—C.G. Jung, Memories, Dreams, Reflections

Free us from these self made hells
of always having to prove ourselves

—Inscription above my writing desk

Contents

1

Me and Dracula

When I was twelve, Mike Daly and I used to go downtown to the midnight horror movies, and it was there that I experienced for the first time an unexpected and overwhelming emotional intoxication. When up on the screen the vampire's shadow fell across the naked white neck of the prone and beautiful young woman, and he swept down, penetrated her with his teeth and began sucking the vitality out of her body, a rush of warm and dangerous blood trembled through me. It was the paradigm of my earliest ideas of love, having the sort of compulsive power that can only be generated by an inner vacuum. Yet a power nonetheless, a primal power or hunger that no analysis can completely encompass, no morality contain, no amount of enlightenment or self-sufficiency completely free us from. Sometimes "…beauty is," as Rilke writes,

> …nothing but the beginning of Terror
> we're still just able to bear
> and why we love it so
> is because it serenely disdains to destroy us.
>
> —(*Duino Elegies 9; First Elegy*)

A quarter century later, I see in the vampire's bite, a man's endless hunger for the vitality and sensuality in a woman that he has become cut off from in himself. I see in the image of Dracula bent over the entranced woman and sucking her blood, the inevitable outcome of a man's desire who has been socialized into a hostile relationship towards all things in himself we in our culture call "feminine." [1]

He is left to go through her, to consume and devour her separateness in order to have contact with what he has been forbidden in himself. As the steady popularity of the vampire image attests, there is something very sexy and seductive in this submission and devouring (the roles of which are not necessarily determined by gender). *Our notions of romantic love sponsor a similar form of attachment to others where we are most self-estranged.* But it gets a lot less sexy after the opening scenes, as I have found again and again in my adult relationships. And so I have been led back inside, often through loss and dreams, to the places I have most abandoned and rejected myself.

As men, we have been *expected* to abandon and repress ourselves in order to live up to a code of masculine stoicism and performance. But the psyche's own psychological remedies prescribed through the dream imagery, provide ways for healing into more wholeness.

The Shaman who came to me in a disco in a dream (Chapter Five) to lead me into the cave of myself has replaced Dracula as my totem for love. It begins by taking the overpowering energy flowing out of the vacuum of the self and into the image of woman, success, addiction, or some similar obsession and following it back to deeper sources of the self, what Emily Dickinson called, "That fine prosperity/whose sources are/interior" (188, #395). It is less sexy than the vampire hunger for attachment, but in the long run perhaps more beautiful.

Whereas the vampire represents a hungering for and controlling in others what we are cut off from in ourselves (i.e. the condition of being self-alienated and externalized), the shaman symbolizes introversion, awareness of and connectedness to inner processes. It is this inner world that masculine culture (or what many call "patriarchal society") has tended to discourage and even punish in men so they could perform more effectively the roles of provider, protector, and producer—what I call the three P's—at the same time requiring (and rewarding) in women the sensuality, gentleness, nurture, and connectedness to others forbidden men.

---

1.   For the woman, the stereotypical move is to submit in order to bond with the man. But, as the poet Pam Obst remarked, "We feed on being fed on. Sustaining another life with our own blood gives us the power over someone else's life." This is, unfortunately, all too true, and brings to mind something Warren Farrell cites from Lawrence Diggs in *The Myth of Male Power*: "The weakness of men is the facade of strength; the strength of women is the façade of weakness" (27).

The shaman has for millennia been the soul healer of a tribe, the witch doctor and spiritual visionary. According to Jungians Robert Moore and Douglas Gillette, "The shaman in traditional societies was the healer, the one who restored life, who found lost souls, and who discovered the causes of misfortune. He was the one who restored wholeness and fullness of being to individuals and communities...."[2] Over time, the shaman has become "the archetype of awareness,...the archetype that governs what is called in psychology 'the observing ego'" (*King, Warrior* 106), that part of us not ruled or restricted by familial or social roles, ego defenses or fears—it is the watcher within that is able to observe ourselves without getting caught up in our masks, personas, and reactions to people and situations. The shaman symbolizes the attentiveness and introversion necessary for reconciling us with what we have become alienated from in ourselves through familial and social prohibitions.

A man is often taught to by-pass the deepest part of his relationship with himself in order to succeed in the hierarchy of power relationships outside himself, in order to survive in our economy, in order to act professionally (or write a book)—or achieve social status or power that unconsciously is his token with which to get someone else's love, since there is little initiation in our culture for his learning to love himself.

Of course, this stoic self-restraint is often a necessary part of getting any job done. The problem comes when it is the core of a man's socialization, and eclipses other less goal-oriented ways of relating to himself and others. This results in an inner emptiness and estrangement that he has not been prepared to relate to, and thus not able to transform. On the contrary, he learns—through a culture addicted to external forms of distraction, or through an emotionally absent father or through our culture's idealization of women as sensual-sexual nurturer, to try to get someone or something else to fill his inner emptiness rather than relate to it consciously, a practice that further alienates him from himself—his true capacity for life—and perilously locates his source of security and self-esteem outside himself. All sorts of self-destructiveness and violence result from this dynamic.

The central problem of male self-alienation begins with the expectation that men take on the roles of producer, performer, authority in ways that preclude having a conscious, receptive relationship to other needs and feelings in

---

2. *King, Warrior, Magician, Lover: Rediscovering the Archetypes of the Mature Masculine* 110.

themselves, and to these in others. *Put simply, the basic problem of masculine culture is the elimination of the personal—for profession and performance.* This is one reason we have traditionally valued—and at times become perilously dependent on, both as individuals and as a society—women's expected role of being emotionally present and nurturing for us when we have found to our utter dismay that, while having become such stoic performers, we don't know how to be with ourselves. *When we become externalized in order to establish ourselves as successes, we hold others hostage to the vacuum we create within.*

It seems remarkable to me that the initiatory guidance I had been lacking from family and culture was provided to me in the form of dream after dream that kept waking me up to my predicament and the prospect of transformation, though I was not yet ready to understand them. My studies of dreams in a clinical psychology program at The Evergreen State College in Olympia, Washington, with dream specialist Dr. Richard M. Jones (*The Dream Poet*), and my interning as a psychotherapist, had attuned me to the peculiar language in which dreams often speak, and their uncanny capacity to mirror in miniature the most important dramas of our lives.

These dreams are records not only of what I became alienated from in myself growing up male; they mirror what many men have become estranged from in themselves through their experience in the family and a culture that too often asks boys as a rite of passage to manhood to repress whatever interferes with maintaining the image of control and authority they are shamed for not living up to: the infant son who drowns in front of his oblivious business suited father, the lover on his way to his girlfriend's house carrying sleeping moles in traps because he doesn't want these parts of his disowned self to get in the way of the image he thinks he needs to live up to in order to keep *her* love; the owl who comes to the middle of the dark forest bearing the man's soul when he has tried to find it in his attachment to a woman; the shaman in the disco; the wounded cat who shows the man that only by relating receptively to his wounds will they begin to heal; and the relief that unexpectedly comes with the wound when it penetrates our ego defenses and interrupts the infantile identification with another—our attempt to make someone else responsible for our well being.

To the extent masculine consciousness—and social status—has depended on controlling outcomes in the external world, we are more likely to become estranged from our inner landscape. This stoicism invites us into a denial of our spontaneity and vulnerability, alienating us from ourselves and isolating us from others. The denial that we are wounded, and the cultural prohibition against woundedness, is the deepest wound of all, because it precludes the awareness and receptivity that leads to growth. This is why dreams have become so central to psychotherapy: our dreams still remember what has become unconscious in us, what we are estranged from and rejecting in ourselves.

One of the fundamental truths that emerges from studying these dreams is that when we seek (as I so often have) to attach to someone else at the places we are most self-estranged or have abandoned or are hostile to in ourselves, loss or a wounding is often the mode of the soul that calls us back into a more conscious and intimate relationship with ourselves. *Without it we can't be on intimate terms with any body else.* When we try to by-pass our shadow, it falls on those closest to us in the form of unconscious projections. And when we seek to disown our shadow or wounded self in a relationship to someone else, the psyche intervenes, often in the form of dreams—to wound us into the more conscious relationship we need to be having with ourselves.

My sub-title, "Men, Isolation and Intimacy" indicates a relationship between a man's socialization that leads to isolation, and how this relates to his experience of intimacy with others. As I suggest in the final chapter, "Love requires of us the ability to surrender our ego needs to the greater ideal of union with another; this first necessitates that we can surrender our ego *defenses* to a greater awareness of and intimacy with ourselves." This deeper awareness is, above all, what the dreams are interested in, and this crisis is what brings about the visit through the dream by the shaman. It is a crisis articulated not only in my life and dreams, but played out with often tragic consequences in masculine culture.

My underlying thesis is that when a son experiences his father and other men as emotionally and physically unavailable, it doubles his dependence on his mother, and women thereafter. From his father's absence, inexpressiveness, or critical distance he not only learns not to rely on men for emotional nurture and support, he learns not to rely on himself. He internalizes the estrangement from father and men as something wrong with himself—something inadequate at the core of his humanity, **and this maroons him somewhere between his father alienation and his mother dependence.**

The absence of the father, uncle, grandfather or mature and self-aware male elder makes it all the more difficult for the son to separate from the mother and the dependencies of childhood. With the mother complex unresolved and his self-image wounded, he enters intimacy with a woman unable to stand his own ground, unconsciously ready to enmesh with her as infant and then distance and cut off from what suddenly feels like a terrifying and shameful loss of self. (This see-sawing in a relationship back and forth between emotional distancing and enmeshing I call the dance between the iron man and the infant.)

Because of his socialization into the masculine code of stoicism and silence, a man's deepest wounds often remain most unconscious, which prevents him from healing into a greater intimacy with himself and others. (What is said here about men is potentially as true for women, especially now that traditional gender roles are undergoing such dramatic change, with women increasingly taking on roles—and psychological characteristics—that were once the province of men.)

One thing I've learned about writing: it's like mowing lawns and making the bed—it's never finished. It is much the same with our ideas about things. No sooner have we formulated our conclusions than the process of coming to them has brought us beyond them. The writing of this book has helped me see the trap of seeing men and women in terms of masculine and feminine. These qualities arise as much from a culture as they do from a gender. A serious appreciation of how men and women are socialized differently ultimately enables us to appreciate the primacy of the individual. The more fully aware and expressed we are as individuals, the less we are constructed by gender socialization.

The deeper we go into ourselves as individuals, the less distinctions such as "masculine" and "feminine" matter, the less our gender socialization or familial experience constructs who we are. But we must first become aware of how we are constructed by familial and gender roles, taboos and expectations, and this means becoming conscious of what transpired in us when we were too young and unconscious to bear witness to the earliest formation of the self. This is important to know, since what we are alienated from in ourselves, we are likely to want to possess, control, or shame in another. *What we don't know about ourselves falls like a shadow on those closest to us in the form of unconscious projections.* It is up to each of us, in our own way, to become conscious of and heal what our socialization and family experience has set us apart from in ourselves. And to this end, dreams remember what we have forgotten.

*   *   *

This book began as a doctoral dissertation in the English Department at The University of Washington, initially titled "Love and the Dehumanized

Man: A Critique of Masculinity" in which I set out to explore—via literary texts—how men become self-alienated trying to become successes, and then take this alienated self to women to be healed, loved. I was interested in how a man will often passionately seek a relationship to a woman or profession rather than develop a more soulful relationship to himself, and how this was reinforced by our ideas of love, our culture and economy.

Though my early reflections on masculinity in literature were articulate and interesting to me, the issues remained at arm's length, visible only in a novel's characters that were, it seemed, the only legitimized subjects. *In retrospect, it was easier to be eloquent about male alienation when I was still writing as if it had nothing to do with me.* Later, after reading Robert Bly's *Iron John* I couldn't go back to pretending that these issues were more alive for the fictitious characters I'd been examining than they were in my own life. I had turned a corner and needed to acknowledge this in my work. Not long after, I began meeting with other men—in men's groups and at the Men's Wisdom Council of Seattle, and this began to shift my locus from exclusively literary texts to men's lives, my own included.

When I started writing, I was faced with a problem that unexpectedly took me years to resolve. I was trying to write about masculinity while excluding my own experience as a man, a person. I was following the conventional code of academic writing (and "profession" in general) which was first and foremost to locate authority outside personal experience, in the seeming objectivity of texts or theories or professional protocol. To include personal experience or sentiment, or a personal relationship to the subject was somehow less legitimate than theory, somehow embarrassingly naïve and unsophisticated. This is to some extent a wise corrective to the potential perils of self-absorption, but the cure can end up being worse than the disease. It finally occurred to me that this was part of the problem of masculinity (and the world and economy we'd created) in the first place, that to "get the job done" and "be a man" you had to separate the job, the performance, from your feelings, personal experience, your body, spontaneity and sensuousness. By locating authority in literary texts at the exclusion of my own "story," I had been writing about male self-alienation in a way that was itself self-alienating. I had come much closer to my subject than I ever intended.

I realized that if I continued writing and thinking about masculinity while ignoring my own experience as a man, a son, a boy, I would be contributing more to the problem than the solution—since to maintain the pretense of objectivity and authority at the cost of a personal relationship to one's work is perhaps the most problematic requirement of masculine culture to begin with.

I guardedly began to accept that my experience as a man, a son, a boy, a lover was going to be central to my study of masculinity and intimacy—much like the modern physicist has accepted that the experimenter is inescapably part of the experiment. Without this sort of self-awareness, we proceed on inevitably erring in our view of ourselves and the world—no matter how coherent our theories are—because whatever we don't understand about ourselves exponentially distorts how we see other things. The dreams I began *having* and *remembering* during the first several years of writing about literature eventually became the basis of this book.

Because the discussion broadens here into the nature of dreams and their relevance to our lives, before it focuses in on masculinity, some readers may want to skip to the next chapter. Though they may also want to come back at another time.

Making Room for Dreams

O God! I could be bounded in a nutshell
and still count myself a king of infinite space
were it not that I had bad dreams.

—Hamlet (II, ii, 263)

Normally I would wish you pleasant dreams, but in this
case, bad dreams would be more helpful.

—Captain Picard to Data

(in the television show *Star Trek: The Next Generation*, when Data is sensing in his nightmares the

presence aboard the ship of an otherwise undetectable bacteria fatal to humans.)

A dream is an answer to a question we haven't learned how to ask.

—Fox Moulder *(*Television show *The X-Files)*

The myth is the public dream and the dream is the private myth.

—Joseph Campbell *(The Power of Myth)*

Even though it took place in sleep, the dream was an effective ritual.

—Thomas Moore (*Care of the Soul* 12)

This they tell, and whether it happened so or not
I do not know; but if you think about it, you can
see that it is true.

—Black Elk, on the story of Bison Woman,
(*Black Elk Speaks* 3)

When I read the above words—spoken by Black Elk to conclude the telling of the myth of the White Bison Woman—I found myself unaccountably attracted to the mood between the lines. They were spoken by a medicine man—a shaman, the soul healer of the Oglala Sioux tribe. How different is his tone from the adversarial, authoritative tone I learned to adopt as a man in our industrial strength tribe and as an intellectual in graduate school. Just the fact that he says, "I do not know" shows a receptivity to things that is hard to come by when we feel pressured to perform and compete

Whether or not something actually happened in this realm of space and time, in "the real world," isn't important to the soul healer; what is important is how the event might be true as an inner event, true, necessary, and important on the symbolic level—the language of the soul, the language of the part of ourselves that is on a spiritual and psychological journey and isn't always part of the literal, material world, and so these events often manifest or come to us between the seams of the known or interpreted world, in trances, visions, reflection, intuitions, dreams and even daydreams—all the modes of awareness that material pragmatism and efficiency encourage us to devalue and do away with. These are the resources we lose touch with on our material quest for happiness.

Dreams are primordial psychological events, dramas enacted without the normal limitations of time, space, social, moral or self-censorship. Dreams come to us between the seams of our structured lives, our conscious selves. The tighter we structure our lives, that is, the more rigid our ego boundaries and defenses, the less open we are to their language, and the more twisted will be their route into our awareness. Freud calls this psychological dynamic "distortion" in *The Interpretation of Dreams* and Jung has referred to it as "compensation."[3] When we are opposed to unconscious content, "bad dreams" are, as Captain Picard says to Data in the earlier quote, "more helpful" than good ones—because they force us to reckon with the resisted material.

Shamanic soul healers of many cultures and tribes knew this long ago and valued dreams as windows to the heart of things, whether to the destiny of a tribe or to the cause of a person's suffering, physical or spiritual. We have rediscovered the importance of dreams from perhaps a more conscious and scientific point of view through psychology.

Shakespeare—as the Hamlet quote suggests—had a deep appreciation for the ability of dreams to reveal one's true feelings or conscience, especially when we are resisting or hiding them from ourselves. In Hamlet's lament we can hear a respect for the ability of dreams to work autonomously from our conscious self or wishes—one of the most extraordinary and useful qualities of dreams. We could say that dreams are the self or the soul or the unconscious manifesting themselves through less ego-censored modes of awareness. Dreams are pure symbolic experience which mirror the state of what is unconscious in us. They are the friend who tells us what we don't want to hear but need to know.

Dreams estrange us from our familiarity with ourselves in essential ways that lead or force us into deepened awareness. Freud called dreams "the royal road to the unconscious" and Jung considered dreams "the most accurate picture available to us of one's unconscious self" because dreams resist being domesticated or censored by our conscious desires or ego, and thus show the condition of our psyche unobstructed by ego defenses and repression. Yet, as we become more rooted in a scientific-rationalistic view and a technological way of life, we are increasingly pressured to run past our dreams, one of the principal roads to the soul, and this is because we haven't had much use for the soul or dreams in the world we have made.

Dreams must have been the first stories about ourselves, the first telling or re-telling of our experience in symbolic, narrative form. Given the dream's

---

3.   "If the conscious attitude to the life situation is in large degree one-sided, then the dream takes the opposite side. If the conscious has an attitude fairly near the "middle," the dream is satisfied with variations. If the conscious attitude is "correct" (adequate), then the dream coincides with and emphasizes this tendency, though without forfeiting its peculiar autonomy. As one never knows with certainty how to evaluate the conscious situation of a patient, dream-interpretation is naturally impossible without questioning the dreamer" (C.G. Jung, *Dreams* 74).

mechanism of representing both physical and psychological events in abstract, symbolic form, dreams must have been the paradigm of myth and literature itself. Dreams, as they do for modern man, presented our predecessors with a symbolic representation of themselves not of their own making, an involuntary representation or perspective hatched in sleep that compelled them, as dreams compel us, to reflect on experience. In so doing, dreams must long ago have prefigured the function of literature. Such an individual who paid closer attention to dreams would be doing a primordial apprenticeship as a writer, that is as one who represents and reflects upon experience. Later still, such persons as the shaman would read dreams for signs and symbols regarding an individual's, or tribe's, health.

It is impossible to know exactly what our prehistoric ancestors thought of dreams or how they experienced them. Perhaps to a mind less consciously differentiated from nature, dreams seemed less separate from "reality." This would suggest that by developing consciousness so thoroughly along rational, scientific, and utilitarian lines we have polarized conscious and unconscious modes of being perhaps more than in the distant past. What a strange phenomenon, then, to think that dreams would be more foreign to us than to our Cro-Magnon predecessors. This is not to say they understood them any better than we do. To those immersed in myth and literature, dream language is not so foreign.

Many people are leery and even dismissive of their dreams, possibly because we are afraid of the autonomy dreams seem to enjoy in our own heads, afraid of not being in conscious control, afraid of what dreams might show us that we are resisting in ourselves beneath our more acceptable personalities. Jung, who along with Freud, is perhaps the most influential dream theorist in western culture, discusses the primitive fear we have of all things unconscious. In this passage he also frames his view of western culture's attitude toward dreams and the soul, an attitude that hasn't changed much since his farsighted observations of 1938:

> The very common prejudice against dreams is but one of the symptoms of a far more serious devaluation of the human soul in general. The marvelous development of science and technics has been counterbalanced on the other side by an appalling lack of wisdom and introspection. It is true that our religious teaching speaks of an immortal soul; but it has very few kind words for the actual human

psyche….Much older than those relatively recent developments [technology and religion] are the primitive fear of and aversion to everything that borders on the unconscious.

Consciousness must have been a very precarious thing in its beginnings. In relatively primitive societies we can still observe how easily consciousness can be lost. One of the "perils of the soul" is, for instance, the loss of a soul. This is a case of a part of the psyche becoming unconscious again.

—(*Psychology and Religion* 18)

Not only is it true that "[c]onsciousness must have been a very precarious thing in its beginnings," it is a very precarious thing whenever, as individuals, we regress to *our* beginnings, our primitive origins, our unresolved infancy, especially in our intimate attachments to others. This is when we most easily lose consciousness, lose ourselves, and are capable of the most desperate actions.

Perhaps we fear this loss of conscious control in dreams because we experience it as a loss of self, a challenge to our ego version of who we are, a challenge to our authority over ourselves, which implies chaos, dissolution and death. Yet, it is at the very edge of this unfamiliarity with ourselves that we discover the value of dreams for showing us a larger world and getting us to relate to aspects of ourselves we've banished from awareness out of fear, shame, familial or social pressure.

As Jung observes, it is the ultimate aim of the psyche to want to bring into our awareness all contents of the unconscious. For him, the pre-eminent aim of life was "the conscious realization of the unconscious." To this end, the psyche wants us to live out all possibilities of experience, at least in symbolic form, and the dream is the perfect mechanism for this purpose. Fear, confidence, love, hate, loss, hope, rage, sorrow, loyalty, betrayal, success, failure, emptiness, fullness—whatever has become unconscious in us and fallen into our shadow self is exorcised in dreams. Dreams are the remarkably concise texts in which all the characters and action are—potentially—aspects of ourselves which the unconscious is asking us to relate to.

Psychological health is when the individual has opened up to the process of integrating the unconscious into consciousness. This is also consistent with Zen meditation practices, whose aim is a mindfulness about, or making room for, all things within and without. When we stop relating to things, close off, or push them away, the system backs up, gets stuck. Repressing thoughts or feelings creates mindlessness, a vacuum, which the psyche rushes in to fill, often in the form of dreams, nightmares, illness or obsessive behavior.

The more holistic function of dreams offers an effective antidote to the mask of success we think we have to wear to gain acceptance and love—because dreams have no interest in keeping up such appearances. They bring into mind what is not being sufficiently lived out in oneself and what will help restore our sense of wholeness, centeredness, and integrity. If, as I'm suggesting, it is central in traditional American masculine culture for a man to subordinate certain feelings, fears, and needs to the need to perform well as a producer, provider, and protector, then such a man's dreams might provide a useful record of what is being repressed on a more cultural level, and a means of relating to that repressed content, or buried self—in the hope of working it through into awareness, into the collective consciousness, so to speak. This requires a psychological descent.

Joseph Campbell has said that "The myth is the public dream and the dream is the private myth" (*Power of Myth* 40). Dreams can also speak through individuals to a society, a tribe, as shamen well knew. So that private dreams can have the same relevance to others as public myths. After all, the most universal truths are based on the most personal experiences. In *The Hero With a Thousand Faces*, Campbell explains that one of the primary functions of dreams is to provide us with the imagery and symbolism necessary for guiding the evolution of our consciousness and spiritual growth—especially when our family and culture don't provide adequate ritual and symbolic guidance for such initiation and transformation:

> In the absence of an effective general mythology, each of us has his private, unrecognized, rudimentary, yet secretly potent pantheon of dreams...(4).

> It has always been the prime function of mythology and rite to supply the symbols that carry the human spirit forward, in counteraction to those other constant human fantasies that tend to tie it back. In fact it may well be that the very high incidence of neuroticism among ourselves follows from the decline among us of such effective spiritual aid. We remain fixated to the unexorcised images of our

infancy, and hence disinclined to the necessary passages of our adulthood.

In the United States, there is even a pathos of inverted emphasis: the goal is not to grow old, but to remain young; not to mature away from Mother, but to cleave to her.

The psychoanalyst has to come along, at last, to assert again the tried wisdom of the older, forward-looking teachings of the masked medicine dancers and the witch-doctor-circumcisers; whereupon we find…that the ageless initiation symbolism is produced spontaneously by the patient himself at the moment of release.

Apparently, there is something in these initiatory images so necessary to the psyche that if they are not supplied from without, through myth and ritual, they will have to be announced again, through dream, from within—lest our energies should remain locked in a banal, long-outmoded toyroom, at the bottom of the sea [my italics] (11).

We can't leave the dependencies of childhood as long as we "remain fixated on" or unconscious of "the unexorcised images of our infancy." Nor can we begin to realize the wondrous reach of human consciousness without "initiatory images" that guide us through stages of evolution, without some assistance in imagining what is possible. For the most part this sort of guidance often found in tribal or "primitive" cultures has been lost in the grinding gears of a more impersonal economy and world.

My hope is that these dreams will go beyond the personal importance they have had for me and will help others go into and emerge from the darkness of their own self-alienation—the unconscious feelings of father-rejection; shame about needs, fears, woundedness and the consequent isolation; workaholism or alcoholism, drug addiction or enmeshment with others. For these are all symptoms of our earliest self-estrangement. Our childhood is not over for us as long as it holds the key to the wholeness we lost when we let that part of ourselves slip into unconsciousness. Part of the initiation we seek, then, involves a descent, or return to what was lost, only this time consciously. It is a descent into the deeper self which lies under the selves we unconsciously constructed for others. And dreams are the guide; they make us aware, through sometimes frightening and painful "stories," that we are in fact estranged from ourselves. Jung's remark concluding his autobiography (quoted earlier) about his own descent into the unconscious is apropos here:

> In fact it seems to me as if the alienation which so long separated me from the world has been transferred into my own inner world, and has revealed to me an unexpected unfamiliarity with myself.

—(*Memories, Dreams, Reflections* 359)

This descent involves our conscious confrontation with our earliest wounds, fears so deep we would rather hold on to someone or something else to avoid falling into our own depths. But falling in we find the capaciousness that we have inadvertently looked for in our attachments to others and our fixations on outer things. This, above all, is what the following dreams tell of.

I have kept a dream journal for the past twenty years, attempting each time I have a dream to write down the dream details with as little interpretation as I'm capable of, so that the dream is as uncorrupted a document from the deeper self as possible. Each chapter begins with the complete dream text, so that the reader might "have" the dream as well.

2

Happy as a King in a Bean Pod

Depression as the Dead End of Self-Estrangement

And power was contagious in my birth....
Manhood
Spat up from the resuffered pain.
I dreamed my genesis in sweat of death, fallen
Twice in the feeding sea...

—Dylan Thomas, "I Dreamed My Genesis"

The Dream

The sun glares at a low, late afternoon angle. I float listlessly on an inner tube in a big open wooden barrel full of water at the end of a dead end street that stops above the sea. I'm depressed, feeling that my life is going nowhere. I look down the empty streets and sidewalks, squinting in the glaring sun, thinking that everyone else is off at jobs or with other people and I'm alone and depressed and don't know what to do with my life, my time. I notice a father several stairway landings below wearing a gray business suit and tie, standing on a dock with his two year old son.

I'm too estranged to pay much attention to them until, suddenly, I hear a cry and a splash and see the infant boy fall off the dock into the sea. The father seems totally indifferent, and makes no move to save his son who has now sunk under water out of

16

sight. I jump out of the barrel and run down the stairs to the dock where the father stands; I throw off my coat and dive in to save the child, swimming down deeper and deeper, searching for him. The water gets colder and darker the deeper I go, and I start to run out of air. I see the flash of his white body through the green tinted water, and grope frantically, almost reaching his arm. But he slips further down and I can't hold out any more without air. I lunge to the surface gasping in a breath and nearly fainting. The sky has grown cloudy and dark, as if it's about to rain. Still floating in the water, I look over to see the father, surprised that the infant boy is standing next to him dripping wet. "Is he okay?" I ask, noticing that the little boy now has the head and expressionless face of an old man. A wan half smile crosses the father's impassive face, and he answers ambiguously, "He's happy as a king in a bean pod."

*   *   *

The infant son drowns in his father's absence or neglect. A father whose own inner child has drowned cannot save his son from the same fate. When a son experiences his father (and men) as absent, unavailable, or, as in the case of this dream, oblivious to his inner needs and experience, he internalizes it as a way of treating himself, and as a mistrust of the masculine in general, his own included. The lack of nurture and initiation both from the personal father and from the cultural fathers maroons young men at crucial developmental crossroads, where they are likely to feel abandoned, unworthy and alienated from the world.

In "The King in a Bean Pod" dream, the infant son is left to drown in his father's obliviousness while the dream ego is stuck at a dead end, unable in his father's psychological absence to bridge the gulf between childhood and adulthood, unable to get on with his life. So he loiters spiritually, waits, floats feeling lost and depressed, lacking a comfortable identity and a reliable basis for action. This is not to blame the father. It is *his, the son's,* responsibility to become aware of how he has internalized his experience of his father. The dream helps to make conscious what has slipped underwater into unconsciousness; the dream helps revive the inner king drowning at the bottom of the son's psyche.

The Bean Pod dream came to me when I was in my early twenties, having just left college after two years where I was determined to prove myself by becoming a great thinker and writer, probably seeking the approval I never got from my father. But I only succeeded in becoming an isolated workaholic, unintentionally mirroring in many ways my own father.

I left school and the isolation I had turned it into, only to find myself depressed, anxious, at a loss for what to do with my life. I took whatever manual labor jobs I could find in order to survive, and agonized that while everyone else was "on track" I was nowhere. I now see that I had been trying to solve an inner problem by focusing on external things, by searching for the right job or profession or girlfriend, by looking for happiness or fulfillment in external things while by-passing a more conscious relationship to myself. And this was the problem in the first place: I had no idea what a conscious relationship to myself was, having been socialized through dysfunctional institutions and people who were largely unaware themselves. **It is this "witnessing" and recovery of our lost selves that the dream provides through the psyche's process of recycling and presenting to us over and over the issues that remain unresolved in us, or the parts of ourselves that drown in the depths of familial and cultural rejection.**

The dream knew, even when "I" didn't that out of this inner work and increasing self-awareness I would be reconciled with a part of myself that had been drowning in *my* obliviousness and neglect all my life, a part that had been relegated to psychological storage in a bean pod, a part which the dream characterizes as one's inner king.

One of the basic insights of modern psychology is that we end up internalizing the prohibitions and imperatives, the rejection or neglect that we experience in childhood and in our culture (Freud's "super ego" and contemporary psychology's "inner child"). To this end we inherit indiscriminately all that has been denied (not dealt with consciously) in our family and culture. By the time I had this dream, I couldn't go on any more as an obsessive, goal driven workaholic. I'd reached a dead end. But it took me years and years, and some good therapeutic guidance (our age's equivalent of the shamanic soul healer) before I recognized this dead end as precisely the right place to begin by being fully present here with self-acceptance and awareness. This sort of acceptance and awareness of ourselves in the here and now is the very basis of Buddhist teachings and eastern spirituality, the sort of mindfulness that we westerners in our rush to succeed in the outside world have typically dismissed.

In the dream, the drama he witnesses at this dead end of the infant son drowning in front of his oblivious father, is the drama I experienced as my father's son, having drowned in all my needs, fears and dependencies while my father was away on business, so to speak. It is an experience many sons have shared...though not with each other.

Reinforcing one of my central themes, in *Under Saturn's Shadow: The Wounding and Healing of Men*, the Jungian analyst and writer James Hollis observes the importance of the initiatory relationship between fathers and sons, and what is lost when this relationship is missing:

> Today, of course, I know the...tribal elders of our time did not know what it means to be a man either. They similarly were uninitiated and could hardly pass on the mysteries and liberating knowledge they themselves lacked. In my own halting fashion I had tumbled to the necessity of rites of passage from childhood to manhood. Not only are such rites about transition from the dependencies of infancy to the self-sufficiency of adulthood, but equally about the transmission of such values as the quality and character of citizenship, and those attitudes and beliefs that connect a person to his gods, to his society and to himself. Yet such rites of passage withered and passed away long ago. "It has often been said," notes Mircea Eliade, "that one of the characteristics of the modern world is the disappearance of any meaningful rites of initiation." Even the phrase 'rite of initiation" or "rite of passage" may not be understood in our time (16).

Without adequate initiatory guidance, we miss opportunities for depth and transformation, and we end up like the son in the dream, in the prime of young adulthood, depressed and isolated at a dead end, at a loss for how to proceed, cut off from the inner resources and self-esteem that would enable us to negotiate these stages of life. *What would be a point of transformation—if properly acknowledged and guided-becomes a point of arrested development, a dead end.* Psychologists know the value of these points of crisis, as did the ancient Greeks, whose word *krisis* means *to separate, discriminate,* in other words, to become more aware.

The dead end of the dream, properly stewarded and brought into awareness, becomes integral to a rite of passage, an opportunity for confronting the psychic wounds which now hold him back from a more fully expressed life.

The Dead End: Depression

I loafe and invite my soul.

—Walt Whitman, *Song of Myself*

The dreamer dives into the water trying to save from drowning a part of himself he has lost—presumably early on in childhood. When the dreamer is unable to reach the drowning infant, and surfaces to find him on the dock with the head of an old man, he knows something is wrong. The father's quizzical reply that the child is "happy as a king in a bean pod" leaves the dreamer bewildered.

A king wouldn't be happy living in a bean pod; this is an image suggesting that the man hasn't given adequate psychological space to the part of himself—his inner king—that ought to be ruling his life, knows what makes him happy, and therefore what roads will serve him and what roads will lead him to dead ends. The dream associates the king with the child that the father allows to drown: as long as we deny that our infant self is drowning, we leave our inner king or queen cacooned in a bean pod—in a sort of psychological coma—so that it does not preside over our life. When our inner king or queen is in psychological storage, our lives lack direction, meaning, depth.

We find ourselves at dead ends or on paths that have no soul. A descent becomes necessary if we are to recover this deep center from which we have become estranged. We go back to the familiar, the familial, back to the father, the mother, the culture, back to the places in our pasts, in ourselves and in our body where we let our kings drown. And there we go inside.

The dreamer has left college, has no job, and is as unsure of what he wants in life as he is of his ability to get it. His life has reached a dead end. The whole business of surviving in his culture has become meaningless for him, precisely because it has been a business; his culture has been more concerned with economics, survival, performance, image, while neglecting the inner landscape. The father in the dream stands by in a business suit and watches obliviously and uncomprehendingly as his infant son drowns. The father is more prepared for business than for fathering. And business, the profit-driven corporate organization of our time and resources, when it is divorced from a more humane and balanced perception of life, is inadequate and even destructive as the paradigm of masculine culture and the main cultural institution responsible for initiating our young men and women into adulthood.

On one level, the dead end indicates the absence of adequate mentoring and initiating by the father and male elders. Yet for the individual it also represents the end of a way of living that isn't taking him where he needs to go. The dead end represents what the psychologist Andrus Angyal calls "bankrupting the neurosis" (*Neurosis and Its Treatment*), coming to the end of a neurotic or compensatory way of life based more on protecting ourselves from fear and trauma than on the expression of the authentic self. It can also be seen in Jungian terms as the "necessary death of the ego," the death of a personality construct that arose in childhood or infancy to protect us from trauma, yet is now holding us back from other possibilities of life beyond our unconscious infantile expectations and defenses. These now have to be woken up, i.e. we must become conscious of them in order to be liberated from them. According to this view, reaching dead ends is an essential part of encountering our depths and becoming conscious of what is unconscious in us. For instance, for a son to have dealt with his father's emotional unavailability by dissociating from his need for a reliable bond with him, only displaces the need without satisfying it. The early trauma of feeling abandoned and unloved by his father makes it safer (for the infant) to cut off from the need altogether—thereby jeopardizing the possibility of closeness with his father or other men later in life. Such submerged expectations from infancy must be brought into our awareness or they rule our lives.

In the dream, as the dreamer floats on an inner tube at the end of a dead end street, he feels like the depressed Hamlet who has no reliable basis for action:

> How weary, stale, flat and unprofitable
> seem to me all the uses of this world.

> —(I, ii, 129)

Like so many men, the dreamer set out on the road to manhood without first taking or making or having been given the opportunity to find out what made him happy. When no one is there to legitimize the process of inwardness or self-awareness, it is difficult to come into deeper self-knowledge and make the passages from one level to another, whether the passage be separating from the dependency on mother, choosing a calling or profession, or committing to a partner in love. Without this centering and depth we experience life as something that happens to us, as something we can only react to, rather than a situation in which we participate, shape, and have choices.

Spiritual Loitering

In the dream, the young man floats on an inner tube at the end of a dead end street overlooking the sea, an image of spiritual loitering and existential crisis. Yet coming to a complete stop gives him the opportunity to confront the deeper self, the one not so busily concerned with what others are thinking or with the dictates of the super ego—the internalized culture and parental police.

At the dead end we don't make full use of our potential because it is closed for repairs, undergoing deep shiftings and realignment. It is easy to feel dislocated from the rest of the world, depressed, worthless, and at a loss for what to do next. "I look down the empty streets and sidewalks, squinting into the glaring sun" feeling empty and estranged from all things. He starts comparing himself to others, thinking how "everyone else is off at jobs or with other people," and he feels even more inadequate and depressed.

Now that he's stopped compensating and avoiding, some of his core feelings about himself manifest more clearly. This is a difficult time in any one's life. These core feelings are beliefs, projections, and expectations formed at the infancy of our personality which have ruled our lives from unconsciousness up until now. At the dead end, we begrudgingly take our psychological inventory. The most that any one can do at the dead end is to observe oneself, especially the negative beliefs and thoughts about oneself, and see these as projections that originate in our earliest experiences. At this point, we usually need others who are themselves initiated into these depths to help keep us from drowning in the negative projections we are trying to *observe* in ourselves. Out of this inward descent will grow the buds of delight that can't grow while we're so self-alienated. Like the Buddha who sits under the Banyan tree for three years, it is enough for us simply to observe ourselves without judgment. To go forward at this point into a more fulfilled and awake adulthood, means, ironically, to go back to our childhood origins where we formed so many beliefs about our relationship to time, to our bodies, ourselves, and to others. As Stephen Wolinsky puts it, we have to wake up from the "trances" we fell into in the past, before we were conscious enough to know we had choices (*The Dark Side of the Inner Child*).

It is at first a frightening cessation of purposefulness and identity wherein one experiences a loss of certitude, direction, and importance, and feels a piercing sense of isolation. It is as if during these dark transitions we float in a cramped barrel of water while the whole sea lies at our feet, waiting for us to make use of its—and our own—potential.

One way of looking at depression is seeing it as a symptom of self-alienation. We feel unmotivated. We think that something must be wrong with us, that we are defective. The problem, as the dream sees it, is that we are allowing to drown, or have allowed to drown all our lives, the part of us that knows what makes us happy.

If we start to do just anything in order to avoid the discomfort and terror of being at the dead end without direction or purpose, we're just deferring a necessary confrontation with the deeper self. I say this knowing full well that sometimes we need to defer or interrupt these difficult confrontations, especially when we lack sufficient support or guides, such as friends, family or a good therapist. *One of our problems is that we've been taught to be ashamed of the very condition that will eventually be a doorway to our deeper self. "Being" is difficult in a culture that puts so much emphasis on doing.*

In the dream, the king is an image of the part of the man that should guide his life, but since the man has relegated the king to a bean pod, he can't rule his life. This self-alienation has led to depression. The dreamer feels he has no future to look forward to nor present to feel at home in. On top of feeling depressed at the dead end, we might also feel unproductive, guilty and ashamed. The guilt and shame actually preclude the sort of receptive relationship we need to have to our depression that would give it meaning and help get us undepressed. *The worst part of depression is the experience we go through trying to avoid it.*

When the inner king is in a coma, and has been most of our lives, it usually means we have become self-estranged to the point that we need an outside perspective, a guide or guides who can lead us into changing the relationship to ourselves through which we killed our inner king in the first place. Realizing this brings one to a tremendous point of transformation. This is a time when we usually get harder on ourselves, yet it is a time we must do all we can to accept, nurture, and be good to ourselves.

These dead ends become even more prolonged, frightening and alienating to us when we haven't been prepared to expect them as necessary and meaningful parts of our spiritual and psychological growth. We do not receive this sort of preparation in a culture that actively denies the shadow side of life—aging, grief, loneliness, death, the poor and disenfranchised—a culture hooked on glamour, cosmetics, success, quick fixes, painkillers, and sixty channels of non-stop entertainment. So, when we come to a dead end it is a difficult opportunity we aren't necessarily prepared to appreciate, let alone legitimize and make sufficient room for as a transit point to a deeper level of consciousness.

Nowadays, it is even customary for psychiatrists and doctors to prescribe drugs like Prozac and Lithium to treat depression. Though drugs can be essential for helping people get through severe and chronic depression, this "prescription" can become an extension of the fear and self-denial that have brought about the depression in the first place. We can see depression as the state we feel when we are not accepting ourselves, when we are actively avoiding or rejecting deeper content, and when this has become an unconscious, routine part of our personality. Depression usually grows up around our wounds; but, paradoxically, it isn't the wound; it is the state of not feeling our deeper wound; it is the self-alienation we feel when we are estranged from ourselves. The psyche is getting our attention through the depression; we must become conscious of the wound or it won't heal.

Faust

The dream of the dead end recalls many such dead ends in western literature, stuck places where proceeding on with life involves a crisis of deepening one's awareness. Hamlet searches for some moral conviction larger than revenge, and for some way of coming to terms with the crisis of his mother's "infidelity." His current turns "awry and lose[s] the name of action." Dante, having "strayed from the right path," finds himself "alone in a dark wood." Goethe's Faust reaches a dead end that leads him to the edge of suicide, where he becomes an initiator into depths that his cultural mythos was failing to adequately examine.

In Faust we find the prototypical masculine dilemna, the quintessential male ego questing after success and becoming isolated within the walls of his own ego to do it, yet convinced he must do so in order to prove himself worthy of love. The double binds can be agonizing.

Goethe wrote Faust in the late 1700's and early 1800's. Already the goal-driven male in western society was experiencing a loss of soul—and it took a poet to really notice this. Faust has come into his middle age deeply unfulfilled by his many accomplishments. He has mastered the major disciplines of his day: philosophy, science, theology and medicine. Yet he is depressed. That's not what Goethe calls it, but the symptoms are the same: a creeping sense that life is no longer an adventure, a predictable horizon causing loss of motivation, isolation, emptiness, a feeling that whatever our current unbearable situation is, it won't change. One begins to go through the motions, fulfilling a routine that has ceased to feed deeper needs. Faust finds himself—professionally—at the top of several fields yet not meaningfully connected to anyone or anything, and least of all to himself. He reaches for a vial of poison to kill himself, but the sound of human voices singing Easter songs outside breaks him out of his trance, reminding him of the possibility of hope and resurrection.

In *Transformation: Understanding the Three Levels of Masculine Consciousness*, the psychologist Robert A. Johnson describes Faust's struggle with the necessary death of the ego as one we all share when we choose the path of consciousness, transformation and growth:

> One day when his feelings of loneliness and meaninglessness reach an unbearable point, he reaches for the poison. This is a terrible moment in the life of an intelligent man. He now sees that his level of consciousness, his perspective on life, will not support him…(54). It is a compliment of the highest order when a man finds that he cannot go farther and that his life is an irredeemable tragedy. His ego consciousness is stalemated, and this stalemate is the only medicine that will drive him out of the Hamlet tragedy and inspire him into new consciousness. A fault of this magnitude cannot be repaired, but can be healed only by finding a whole new level of consciousness from which to function…(55). The fact that our culture has lost most of its guidelines for people at this point of their evolution makes it all the more difficult (58).

The death of the ego is a frightening time in one's life, especially in a culture that rewards the appearance of certainty and productivity and positive thinking more than it does the darker modes of the soul where we often find more depth.

As a once popular song puts it, "Accentuate the positive/Eliminate the negative." The misguided project of "eliminating the negative" is what puts us in a position of having to "accentuate the positive" in the first place. It's only when we use the positive to deny the negative, or the external to deny or avoid the *internal*, that we have to try so hard to inflate it, "accentuate" it, externalize it.

Well, Faust tries to do this, tries through the agency of Mephistopheles' magic to find happiness in external things, through romantic love with a beautiful woman. But this doesn't bring him inner peace or fulfillment. His alienation and estrangement only increase as he attempts to find fulfillment through ambitious accomplishments in the world, in an important position in the Imperial Court, through military victories, and finally through a vast reclamation project in which he attempts to prove, among other things, that his will and perseverance can master Nature. (This recalls a similar quest by a certain Captain Ahab.) Throughout, he is aided by Mephistopheles' supernatural powers, which become dramatic analogies to the effect the external quest for money, power, fame and material success can have on one's inner life. Faust succeeds by industriousness, dikes, dams and magic to reclaim a long stretch of coastal land that lies beneath the sea. But his self-made "kingdom" is interrupted by a small parcel of land, "high ground" owned by an elderly couple, which existed before Faust's ambitious reclamation project, and stands as an irritant reminding him of things lying outside his control, his grasp, his *ego*. He tries to buy them off their land, offering a huge estate in exchange, but they are happy in their humble cottage, and content to live out their last days simply. Finally, their contentment threatens the whole foundation of Faust's ego, his quest for fulfillment a la the manipulation of external things, and he directs Mephistopheles to forcibly evict them from their land. (Part of the symbolism here is the attempt to "eliminate" aging.) In the process, Mephistopheles' murders them. This brings Faust crashing down inwards.

In the night, he is visited by four gray hag spirits, one of whom takes away his sight. Like Oedipus before him, Faust is physically blinded to the outer world. Then and only then does he begin to see the important events he has been overlooking *on an inner level*. When he stops looking outward, seeking fulfillment through his ego quests and makes a place for soul and compassion *in himself*, he begins to experience fulfillment and inner peace. We encounter a similar opportunity at the dead end in the dream, "Happy as a King in a Bean Pod."

In the dream, the dreamer's road ends where the sea begins. There is no place for him to go back to and only the sea sparkling in the glaring sun before him. He is at a dead end that he can't get beyond as long as he's cut off from a vital part of himself, which the dream characterizes as the drowning infant and king in a bean pod. The dreamer's ego structure has developed around the drowning or repression of the inner child, and so it must be transformed if he is going to save his inner child-king from drowning.

The dreamer floating on the inner tube is an image of receptivity and surrender—not quite stasis. A deep body of water in a dream almost always signifies one's transformative depths. He has stopped trying to control and prevail over his situation. Perhaps the "inner" tube signifies the inner part of ourselves that keeps us afloat when we let go of the external things like people, jobs, schedules, goals and personalities that we normally rely on to give our lives definition and meaning. Sometimes, like Faust, we need to be stripped of all our paraphernalia of personality and importance before we get down to a deeper level of being.

The Play's the Thing
(Wherein I'll Catch the Conscience of the King)

The dream ego in the Bean Pod dream has come to a dead stop and a curious thing happens. Just when he thinks he'll be at this dead end forever and he'd rather be dead, a drama is played out before his eyes the meaning of which can free him from his isolation and despair. It is as if the dream has brought the dreamer to a front row seat to witness the drama about how and why he arrived at this dead end in the first place.

He sees a man's infant son fall into the water, and sees the father do nothing to save the infant. If we read this dream as an allegory of the dreamer's infancy and childhood, it seems that the time has come for him to act in order to save this part of himself from drowning.

The father seems strangely cut off from the reality and urgency of the moment. His face is characterized by absence, impassivity, yet there is immense grief and woundedness underlying his effort to be so controlled and self-possessed. *The father stands on the dock in his suit and tie while his naked son drowns before his very eyes. He doesn't understand that his son is drowning, psychologically speaking, just as he was unconscious when he himself drowned as an infant in his father's shadow.* Such self-alienation can be handed down for generations, until men from several generations stand around in business suits afraid of getting wet, even while one of their sons drowns—gets drug addicted or commits suicide—right under their noses.

The father wears a business suit and avoids the water, even if his son or inner son is drowning in it. The business suit calls attention to business and how it is conducted in our society: the man's time, body and mind, his inner needs and his connection to these in others become subordinated to productivity, profit and the time clock. In the dream, the business suit symbolizes all that the man has had to disown in himself—let drown—in order to do business, conform to the corporate order, fit into the hierarchy of economic relations, be a man

The dream may well describe many men's experience of their father: that he stood on the dock in his business suit seemingly oblivious to the fact that they were, metaphorically speaking, drowning in the shadow of his emotional absence, their father hunger, their mother dependence, their need for fathering never answered. It is not necessarily the father's fault. *If his own inner son has drowned he cannot save his son from the same fate.* In fact, he probably experienced the same thing with his own father and will unconsciously perpetuate the same fate for his son, especially when he is encouraged by his culture to do so.

The business suited father represents a masculinity that's totally divorced from the inner life, from water and his transformative depths, from the unconscious, divorced from and oblivious to the inner child and his needs—and this speaks of a serious problem with masculinity and fatherhood in our culture. The father wears a business suit and doesn't want to get wet. And, once again, his son is naked and needy. Repression of the infantile self has polarized the psychological content, creating dualities in the psyche: the iron man and the infant.

When the fathers learn to stay away from water and any feelings associated with infantile needs and fears, these merely get preserved in an unconscious, unevolved, infantile state. Simultaneously, false identities are created to compensate for what is being repressed. So he avoids water, and his son—both inner and biological—metaphorically drowns in whatever fears and needs he negates, shames or is unavailable for. Then as sons we go on to internalize this neglect.

The King

The dream ego in "Happy as a King in a Bean Pod" "floats listlessly on an inner tube in a big wooden barrel full of water at the end of a dead end street overlooking the sea." *At this place of inaction, he encounters the submerged parts of himself without which he can no longer go on living.*

The dream makes the point that this inner child is of great value and is lost at a great cost. The father himself makes a cryptic remark that associates the child with a king. His remark is perhaps the key to the whole dream and to the dreamer's experience of being isolated at a dead end. As Robert Bly says of the inner king: "A man whose king is gone doesn't know if he has the right to decide even how to spend the day" (*Iron John* 111).

The young man in the dream surfaces from his descent to save the child and sees him dripping wet next to his father, with the head and face of an old man as vacant and expressionless as the father's. When he asks the father if the child is okay, the father betrays the truth even while trying to deny it: "He's happy as a king in a bean pod." This is clearly a euphemistic way of describing the child's condition. The infant son falls into the sea of his father's absence—and comes up as an old man without any feelings, only a vacant gaze; something tragic has happened. Something vital has been lost: we grow old impassively—we die young when we let our inner king drown. And the unavailable father is a vital part of the drowning.

A king wouldn't be happy in a bean pod. A king wants a kingdom. The king gives the kingdom meaning as the guiding, connective principle of the kingdom, the individual's life. It is the image of the part of the self that can transform our life and world into a meaningful cosmos. *The king is an archetype symbolizing, among other things, the integrated self: all the various parts or identities of oneself harmonize through the unifying principle of the king because the king focuses the energies of the kingdom, not for himself, but for the overall good. When a king doesn't act for the good of the kingdom, he is not a king but a tyrant.* Bly also links the king symbol to a "transcendent cause" (Iron John 151).

But the man has not given the child enough room in his life for him to have a kingdom. Rather, the king has been cacooned in a bean pod, not dead yet not living either. This is the consequence of allowing our inner child to drown. The child drowns very quickly, and, as the dream reveals, at a very early age. Our unbounded enthusiasm for more and more life as kids can be drowned out of us in one long terrifying dip under the water of the adult's neglect or shame or abuse. So that when we come back up, we've lost our vitality, our spirit, our self-esteem, and our lives head toward dead ends. Fortunately, in the dream, drowning is a metaphor.

The kingliness or queenliness we feel at birth is to us as we grow older an almost unfathomable and forgotten reality. So fragile is it in the life of a child, and so hungry are children to have their needs met, their interests approved and encouraged, watered like buds with the adult's attention, that simple neglect can kill this remarkable purity and diamond-like lucidity of the child's knowing, and the next thing you know, they have the blank stare of one whose dreams are dead.

That the child is being associated with the king is surprising when we think of kings as magisterial authority figures. And it suddenly seems naive and sentimental to think that the dream is asking us to consider the child as the proper king of the man's life. But it makes sense when we think of the inner child as that part of ourselves that knows what most deeply engages us, and would rule our lives accordingly. Regal status may impress us, but it does not impress the psyche, which seeks only the full expression of the self, not power over others. So if the child in us knows what makes us happy and what activities will most fully absorb and express our energy, then this is the identity, according to the dream, that ought to rule—or guide—our lives. The dream isn't necessarily equating the child with the king; the symbology is not so literal; yet their fates are intertwined: if the child is drowning, the king cannot manifest himself in the man's life.

Children have uncorrupted instincts for wonder and play, for a spontaneous, animal-intuitive connection to their bodies and nature, for being spontaneously absorbed in the wonders of the world, and for unselfconsciously expressing the truth of their feelings. They hum and sing and make up impromptu songs as they play along. Twenty years later they'll be afraid to be overheard whistling in an elevator.

When we are raised to be competitors and successes, we don't have time for wonder or to be unselfconscious about the truth. We wear the armor of status and ego, which protect us from the idea of shame and "failure," yet cut us off from our natural affinity with all things. Thus it often takes a fall from great rank and status—as Oedipus, Faust, and King Lear discover—before we are reconciled with our deepest truths, our deeper self, and ultimately with these in others.

There is such power in the child, yet it has no power to make boundaries with those on whom it depends. A child has no choice but to do all it can to win the love of the adults around it, even if it means a sort of emotional suicide or death of the wonder and pleasure-seeking self. Fortunately, those deaths don't have to be permanent

So the buried child carries with him the man's ability to play and wonder; he knows what makes him happy. But he also carries with him the man's deepest fears from infancy and childhood. No wonder we don't see the buried child much after the son leaves adolescence. This is also why we see so few adults who still spontaneously express or have access to their inner child.

The dream provides the appropriate image in the form of the child-as-king of the man. The father doesn't say, "He's happy as a king in a casket," or "He's happy as a sardine in a sardine can." He says, "He's happy as a king in a bean pod." The bean pod is an embryonic image suggesting that the king is still alive in a green growing, organic container or cacoon. It is an inadequate space for the king to preside over the man's life, but the king isn't dead. It is as if the king is in a coma, dormant in the drowning child, but accessible at any time if we will give our "childish" needs and feelings more room in our conscious life. The bean pod image suggests that the man can begin to nurture the space the king is suspended in.

The symbol of the king carries with it the principle of centeredness, the ability to act for the good of the kingdom, that is, for one's whole self. If we look at the king as emblematic of psychic health, the king has power only in so far as he has the welfare of the kingdom, i.e. the whole self, in mind. Ultimately, the king symbolizes an integrated personality, a center and axis around which revolve the various activities, interests, and identities of the self. The king is the center that holds together all of the man's contradictions, passions, dreams, grief. The king is the container large enough to hold everything without falling apart or denying—repressing—anything. It also symbolizes the man's strength and coherence in the presence of others.

The presence of the king as an archetype shows that the man's life is ordered in a meaningful way, structured around deeply felt values. In *Iron John*, Robert Bly, who has written extensively about the king image or archetype, clarifies this relationship between the child and the king:

> The presence of the king says the space is sacred—a cosmos rather than a chaos….Wiping out kings severely damages the mythological imagination. Each person has to repair that imagination on his or her own (109).

> The inner king can make clear what we want without being contaminated in his choice by the opinions of others around us….When we were one or two years old, the inner King, we would guess, was alive and vigorous. We often knew what we wanted and made it clear to others. For most of us, our King was killed early on (110).

> A child has a mood. The grown ups have bigger moods. By the time a child is twelve, he doesn't know what his mood is any more. A

man whose king is gone doesn't know if he has the right to decide even how to spend the day…(111).

The process of bringing the king back to life, when looked at inwardly, begins with attention to tiny details—catching hints of what one really likes.…What were the delights we felt in childhood before we gave over our life to pleasing other people?…I would say that, after attention to tiny desires, the next step begins not with resolutions, but with a long grieving over the dead inner King, surrounded by his dead warriors.…The inner King, once recovered, requires feeding and honoring if he is remain alive, and each man or woman has to figure out how to do that for him or herself (112).

When we discover that our king or queen is dead, i.e. that we are not living the life we want, we must go through a descent of sorts—the diving into deep water—to reach the king which now lies buried under the wounds of our childhood rejection and denial, and the defensive strategies that we built around these wounds. So—except for those fortunate ones whose king or queen was nurtured early on by the parents—we reach the king through some form of conscious grieving, through our childhood wounds. Where we are most wounded is where we buried our gold, our more authentic, less ego defended self. Making room for the awareness of these wounds is the first step to recovering our cacooned inner king. Perhaps as we grieve over what has been lost in us, we simultaneously become more attuned and attentive to the little things that make us happy, no matter how silly or seemingly insignificant the things are that give pleasure or pique our curiosity.

With the thawing out of our deeper self come many associations, memories, joys, longings and losses. Our grief and joy intensify simultaneously because they have been under water, dormant in the drowning child. As Bly says, the process "begins not with resolutions, but with a long grieving over the dead inner king" (112). This sequence is born out in the dream: the dreamer reaches his lost king only after diving into the depths of his wounded childhood, his unavailable father. Perhaps in the beginning of this process of recovering one's king, then, the man or woman will be watering the buds, the bean pod, with his or her own tears.

3

The Men's Room
and the Great Horned Owl

Losing His Lover and Finding His Soul

Just a glimpse into the ladies room as you watch your girlfriend go in shows this fancy couch, and usually a mirror with
a nice wooden frame and a boudoir or stand.

You go into the men's room and there's piss on the floor, and
the mirror is some unbreakable metal thing that looks like it
came from a carnival fun house—you know, the kind that
totally distorts your features.

—Roy Pettus, friend,
in conversation

The Dream

*I'm leaving the home my girlfriend and I have shared for five years. As soon as she's
gone I'm devastated, even though I initiated the break-up. Night has fallen and I've
got to find a place to stay. I feel empty, homeless, and numb. I want to go back to find
her, but I know I can't go back. Half alive, I walk the dark streets looking for somewhere to stay. I phone my oldest brother but he tells me, "We don't have any room.
And besides," he adds in a conspiratorial whisper, "She [his wife] wouldn't like it."*

Hours pass. Weary and exhausted, I wander beyond the outskirts of the city into a dark forest. It is dark and getting colder and I haven't dressed warmly. I just want a place to sleep. Sometime in the middle of the night I see yellow light glowing through the oblique windows of a stone building. When I get up close I see that it's a restroom made of solid granite stones. The door is open, or maybe there is no door, just an open entryway above which are carved the letters M E N. I go in and descend the stone stairs leading underground to a cavernous half basement, like a locker room. Beneath a naked light bulb hanging from the ceiling, I find a hard wooden bench fastened to the wall, and lie down to try to keep the cold off and get a little rest.

At the first trace of twilight, I awaken feeling empty and in a state of shock, with almost no motivation to live, as if by losing her I've lost my ability to feel alive and secure. Perfunctorily, I climb the stairs and step out the doorway. It's still dark, just on the edge of dawn. Everything in the forest is incredibly still, as if listening, waiting for something. Just then I hear the slow, steady beating of enormous wings. The sound reverberates straight to my heart and is somehow reassuring, comforting. I watch in amazed silence as a Great Horned Owl glides past me in the twilight, its wing tip so close it almost touches my shoulder. The bird's presence instantly calms and reassures me; I feel my body relax and warm up again. The owl's presence has hushed the forest, as if the whole world should stop and acknowledge its appearance. For a long moment everything is tranquil, having fallen into place, and for the first time in the dream I feel good being alone.

But as morning breaks, I see in the growing light all around the Men's Room huge yellow dump trucks and bulldozers, men in hard hats ready to continue the job of mowing down the forest. Trees lie broken apart like match sticks, the ground gashed open, the red earth flattened to be covered over with asphalt for a parking lot. I feel sick inside that even this little bit of refuge is being destroyed. The owl is gone, and she is gone, and I feel empty and hopeless in a cold, hostile world.

✳   ✳   ✳

Losing His Lover

I dreamed this in my late twenties when my relationship was ending with a woman I'd been with for seven years. In retrospect, it is easy to see that I was looking outside, to other women mostly, for something I was unable to provide myself, and had been doing this most of my life, putting some "loving" person between me and my unloving relationship to myself. I now see that my passionate and at times desperate search for outer forms of love corresponds to an inner self-estrangement that the dream personifies as the desolate men's room, a room which, I am finally realizing, we disown at great peril to ourselves and our relationships to others.

Like Jung, who described his life's work as "the conscious realization of the unconscious" (*Word and Image* 13), I had "discovered an unexpected unfamiliarity with myself" which I had been avoiding, burying, through relationships to others and especially in "love" or romantic, sexual relationships. The loss of my lover had unearthed this buried relationship to my core self, one that I hadn't been prepared for by any of my childhood experience, guidance from my father or mother, school or boy scouts or football practice or movies and tv—all of which seemed to reinforce a polarization of masculine and feminine behaviors and characteristics, compelling me to censor and stuff in myself what I then went looking for from the mythic beautiful woman.

The dream, then, is about the paradigmatic situation of a man feeling lost and empty, dehumanized even, without a woman's love or attention. It is as if without the security of her companionship and the reassurance of her attention, he falls into the basement of a deeper though at this point frightening relationship to himself. The men's room mirrors the inner landscape we become alienated from in ourselves when we learn early on to be stoic and assertive—to live up to heroic, external images—while banishing other needs and fears to the basement of the self, where they become increasingly forbidding. The men's room in the dream signifies an unreceptive attitude towards ourselves. Our resulting self-estrangement makes it feel easier to try to fill this void with someone else's attention (or deny our needs altogether). So often the barren and isolated men's room is what lies at the back of men's minds when we censor in ourselves the qualities our culture has designated feminine—softness, receptivity, nurture, sensuality—which we then come to depend on externally in a woman. If the father is not a nurturing presence for the son, this dependency begins with his relationship to mother and gets refracted unconsciously throughout his romantic relationships. Regardless of gender, our self-estrangement leads us to want to fill our inner emptiness with someone else's attention.

When we don't get validation in childhood, or what psychologist Harville Hendrix calls "mirroring" of the whole self from our parents (and later from peers and society), we learn very early to banish aspects of our genuine self to the basement or "shadow" self—the men's room. In Jungian psychology, the "shadow" is all that we are hostile to or unconscious of in ourselves, all that we haven't owned in ourselves. The prohibitions that would cause one to create the shadow self come not only from our family, but from our culture. Hendrix observes that the sort of "selective mirroring" that goes on in the family in the form of rewards and punishment, acknowledgement and shaming, also goes on in our culture according to gender:

> ....all too often this kind of selective mirroring has to do with gender, with boys praised for their assertiveness and stoicism, and girls for their cuteness and helpfulness. The result is that the child, yearning to be whole, develops a false self by identifying only with parentally or socially approved traits.... His energy is limited to the mirrored traits, and those unmirrored traits become his recessive "Lost Self"...an aspect of his "shadow."

> Full and positive mirroring is essential to the child's sense that all of him-whether he is being tender or assertive, silly or smart, Peter Pumpkin or Mr. Jones across the street—is valid and acceptable. If I would have said to Hunter [his two year old son], "That's silly, you're not a dinosaur," I would have interfered with his transient experimentation with a new trait, and he would no longer feel confident of who he was...(*Keeping the Love You Find* 87).

With better "mirroring" or initiation from the parents, and by extension from our culture, these inner spaces wouldn't be so fearful and barren, and becoming a man wouldn't bring with it such widespread inexpressiveness, isolation, and unhealthy dependence on women. We are left, as adults, to parent the inner child, resurrect the lost self, that was incompletely mirrored by the parents—and our culture, and which we have consequently become estranged from. This child carries with it our most uncorrupted instincts for well being, our most authentic self.

The dream is about the difficult beginning of discriminating between this self-estrangement and our attachments to others, i.e., *the dream begins where his relationship with her ends and his relationship with himself begins; that is, where he becomes responsible for his own well being.* Relationships become all the more difficult when we attach to others at the places we aren't on good terms with ourselves, the places we are self-alienated. *The dream seems to be suggesting—through the symbol of the men's room—that this self-estrangement can happen on a cultural level, and according to gender.* The loss of a lover or partner, devastating as it can be, confronts us with the need (or involuntary opportunity) to reconcile with the self we have been alienated from and avoid while seeking someone else's love and attention.

When we are avoiding parts of ourselves in our attachments to others, loss is often the mode of the soul that calls us back to this inmost self. When we lose sight of our inner estrangement and it becomes incomprehensibly entangled in a relationship to someone else, often the only way to clarity is separation—emptying ourselves—at least psychologically—of attachments and purposes and status that we have used to cover up the more fundamental relationship we have to ourselves.

The dream thus describes a necessary descent, an ordeal or dark night of the soul, that is necessary if one is to reconcile with vital parts of oneself he or she has banished from expression, often in accordance with cultural gender taboos.

Without her he feels utterly bereft of inner resources because focusing so intently to succeed on the outside—i.e. cultivating stoicism and control—has left his relationship to himself unsympathetic and inhospitable. *The desolate men's room and the hard hatted men destroying the forest with their yellow machinery symbolize the hostile relationship we can develop with ourselves when we are socialized to be performers, providers and protectors in ways that preclude being receptive and nurturing to ourselves.*

This cold, forbidding, ill-equipped underground room is the only place he finds to spend this dark night of the soul. And yet it is the right place for him because it symbolizes something about his core relationship to himself that the dream is presenting to him to be consciously reckoned with. It is the only place he can begin to change his life on the most fundamental level: the dream begins where his relationship with woman as lover-mother ends and his relationship with himself as nurturer and parent begins. But, as the condition of the men's room and his terror about being alone suggest, he is not very well prepared to provide this nurture for himself. The dream comments on this crisis of self-alienation.

The Men's room in the dream is an image of the dreamer's deeper self, which is at this point unfinished, unlived in, and coldly utilitarian. That it resembles a locker room links it to the informal initiation rites of the locker room—sports, competition—which measure us and teach us to measure ourselves almost exclusively by our external performance. A life of denial and performance can leave this level of the self—this inner room—vacant and forbidding, disconnected from others. It is an all too typical move at this point for us to try to get someone else to fill this inner vacancy.

The descent into the men's room empties the dreamer of outer forms of security and identity, and he experiences a form of the death of the ego.

His brother has no room for him to spend the night of his descent because his brother has made no room for his own shadow. So he can't take in anyone else's. Besides, he tells the dreamer "in a conspiratorial whisper", his wife wouldn't like it if he spent the night. His dependence on his wife precludes his ability to be there for his brother. *She is care taking the part of him that would otherwise be the place in himself he could accommodate his brother's emotional needs.* His brother represents the enmeshed relationship he just left.

In "The Men's Room" dream, the dream ego walks through the city hour after hour finding no comfort for his pain, no place to be. Finally, exhausted, he comes upon a dimly lit building at the edge of a forest. The inlaid stone above the granite entryway is inscribed with the letters M E N. This must be the right place. He has no where else to go, no choice but to descend the stairs. The inscription above the entryway suggests that his predicament is shared by other men.

The men's room shows him what his relationship to himself looks like without the intermediary love of a woman, and so, hard as it is, it is the right place for him to begin.

By the look of the men's room, it appears that his experience of the masculine has not been very sympathetic to his needs. No wonder he has avoided it. Everything in the men's room is cold and hard, purely utilitarian: the hard wooden benches, the cold metal lockers, the stone steps and the concrete walls. It is cold, damp, dimly lit. No couches, chairs, or comfortable places to rest. No warmth, no heat, no flowers, no wall paper, no color. No mirrors: only the rough brushed steel sheeting that once held in place a mirror long since shattered and gone. Perhaps the lack of mirrors means that here, apart from his now lost lover, he cannot see himself, has trouble connecting with himself at this deeper subterranean level. Alone, he feels like he has disappeared, become a ghost, so mediated through her has his relationship to his deepest needs of belonging and security been.

Masculine culture, as it is manifested in the economy of our lives, often makes very little space for joy, sensuality, or *conscious* suffering in a man's life, and thus makes no place for comfort or soul. It is this sympathizing with ourselves and nurturing ourselves that connects us back to others, giving us the sense that we belong to a community. This connectedness to ourselves ultimately connects us to others, to everything on a level far deeper than utility, profit, or ego. In turn, the connection to others takes the pressure off of the ego to be the only conduit for self-acceptance, self-esteem.

If we give ourselves the proper time and attention, we find that our fears aren't as bad as we imagined; it is the fear of fear that makes fear so fearful. We are afraid of fear because we have been brainwashed to be performers who have no fear. There is even a prominent advertising campaign championing the motto: "No Fear." They might as well say "No Growth." It makes it difficult for us to take the time to settle into our depths and into a deeper relationship with others. The rejection of fear and the darker modes of life can be traced to a lack of self-acceptance and the consequent compensating obsession with external images, fantasies of power, beauty, youth, success. Pretty soon we're rejecting wrinkles, old age, and the wisdom that once came with it and was given back to youth through elders. Now our elders are put away in nursing homes where they watch television shows and commercials about how to avoid wrinkles while newscasts describe young men killing each other. "No, Fear."

The men's room shows—to some extent—what is legitimized, encouraged, "mirrored" in a man's relationship to himself by our society: utility, stoicism, what becomes isolation, and yearning for a woman to make us whole again. A man's capacity for self-love isn't mirrored at all. Women have been the only safe container for his experience of needs and vulnerability, especially as an infant when he depended on his mother for survival and rarely experienced his father as affectionate, holding him in his arms, feeding, pampering, and playing silly games with him. As long as the barren men's room and the workmen destroying the forest are his experience of the masculine, of being with himself, he will feel desperately empty when he is alone without a woman. And this won't change as long as we're trapped in the performer mode or other compensating or avoiding behaviors.

We often by-pass this dark opportunity to descend the stairs into a deeper relationship with ourselves, because we have not been prepared to see it as an opportunity.

The dark forest is often a mythological locale for a psychological ordeal or transformation. Things are dark and unfamiliar there, far from the well lit town where everyone knows who we are and we even think we know who we are (i.e. that our ego version of ourselves is the whole picture). So the dark forest far away from the familiar provides the proper conditions for exceeding the uses of our old ego defenses as well as encountering the shadow self we have been estranged from, and which will make us more complete. I've heard Robert Bly speak of the significance of the dark forest in mythology and fairy tales as a symbol for initiation into the deeper self. He says in such a time you go to the edge of the forest and enter where it is darkest. Metaphorically speaking, that's where we're most estranged from ourselves, and most need to be initiated into new awareness. This is also where we became doubly attached to mother when we experienced father and the masculine as emotionally unavailable or unreliable.

Descent in dreams often signifies entering unfamiliar depths of ourselves. In the middle of the dark forest the dreamer finds the men's room and must descend the stairs into a more conscious relationship to his shadow self. This is also where he will find his own inner resources apart from a woman or a lover. Taking total responsibility for one's own well-being is the province of adulthood, though the route by which we get there invariably leads us back to where we became self-estranged in childhood and through cultural taboos and expectations.

The isolated men's room is emblematic of his core relationship to himself, not indicative of the means for healing this self-alienation. Isolating ourselves to find ourselves never works; it only defeats a person. That is just another version of masochistically trying to prove ourselves alone, one of the most wounding imperatives of masculine culture. There is no self-acceptance in that, and self-acceptance is what he needs most of all at this stage.

This place the dreamer has come to looks like he feels inside: heavy and empty. Exhausted, he sinks into the barren depths of himself—a necessary prelude to making these depths more hospitable. He rises from the hard bench, feeling half dead. With leaden steps he slowly ascends the stairs. The night merges with the day, the light slowly blending with the darkness like a river meeting the sea. He feels the forest so quiet, so hushed, as if listening, waiting for something. Suddenly he hears the soft beating of enormous wings coming closer and closer. A huge great horned owl approaches with spellbinding grace, almost touching him with his wing tips. He stands there, mesmerized. It is so graceful and fluid, the man forgets his pain and loneliness and is simply filled with the owl's presence, as if the owl has come to comfort him in his desolation and despair. "For the first time in the dream I feel good being alone." This is the culmination of the dream, the unexpected discovery of inner life at the heart of deathlike loss, the discovery of inner resources in the face of outer loss.

The owl's ability to see in the dark symbolizes for the dreamer his psychological ability to overcome or *see through* this loss, to see the growth within the apparent grief, terror and insecurity that have come with the loss of his relationship with his lover, upon which he had based—*a la* the son-mother dependency—his sense of existential and even corporeal security. He is experiencing a dark time of loss and difficult rebirth, and so he must be able, psychologically, to see in the dark.[1] In some native American and Polynesian traditions the owl is associated with death and the soul, and the soulfullness that often is attained only through the death-transformation of a part of the self. Birds and flight have been associated with spirituality in most mythologies across all ages—from the mythic phoenix rising from the ashes, to Christ and the dove. So perhaps the dream is suggesting that the possibility of the dreamer's spiritual awakening comes also through this dark ordeal in which he begins separating himself from his attachment to others. (Nor does one have to physically leave his or her lover, husband, wife, or partner. It is only essential that one experience these on a symbolic or inner level.)

The owl figure in the dream recalls what many native American Indian tribes refer to as a spirit helper or guide, arrived at only by undergoing a difficult solitary experience, a solo journey, or vision quest, often lasting several days and nights in the wilderness without food. Such rituals frequently accompany a son's initiation into manhood. The difficult truth to come by here is that meeting up with the owl—his soul—is precluded by our attempts to find security and identity in someone else or in external situations.

From this elemental immersion in nature and solitude—guided by the tribal elders—the young man or woman would emerge having contacted, through dreams, visions, or a sign from nature, a spirit helper who will be with him or her throughout a lifetime, becoming a totem or source of inner strength and centeredness, and a reminder that no matter where he is or what he is going through, he is not alone: his experience happens within a meaningful framework described by the tribe's spiritual and initiatory rites. The tribal initiation process shows the young man that he doesn't have to become an isolated ego to prove himself a man or a success; in fact, part of the purpose of

---

1. The psychologist James Hillman uses the notion "seeing in the dark" in *The Dream and the Underworld* to describe the willingness to follow the bridge of dreams inward to the unconscious content, and learn about ourselves and life and death from the angle of the shadow or underworld, rather than from what we already know.

nearly all initiation rites is to teach the individual a quality of conducting one-self—self-reliance, courage, sacrifice, acceptance of pain—in the context of community and through the bond or bridge connecting the young to their elders, life to death, grief and pain to joy and hope. This opens up the self to sources of help outside the ego, and reinforces the bond between self and community, self and other, so that some day the son will mirror his elders' concern for his well being toward himself as well as toward others. In this sense, our culture—partly due to an economy that is often antithetical to the needs and cohesiveness of the community—is failing to provide our young with adequate role models which help them navigate difficult life stages and existential crises. When we can't face the crisis, we lose out on an opportunity for growth. Respect for and connection to the older generations diminishes or completely disappears, and the bridge gets washed out between childhood and adulthood, psychologically stranding the sons in this no-man's land in a dark wood where they get depressed, crestfallen and sometimes very, very angry.

The geography of this descent constitutes a gradual and necessary estrangement from the familiar self.

We learn to see in the dark only when we're lost, only when we're forced to strain our eyes, our capacity. As Kierkegaard said, "These are the only genuine ideas, the ideas of the shipwrecked." Many of our resources we don't know we have until we are forced to make use of them. But without some mentoring, this opportunity to access these resources that the owl symbolizes will be lost, and the individual overcome by the terror, to which he reacts instinctively through the reptilian brain by either fighting or fleeing—fight or flight. When we lack guidance, we have little choice but to remain unconscious. *The lack of timely, reliable mentors leads to the shame and isolation of the men's room.* The men's room dream represents another developmental chasm that the son has immense difficulty transiting without helpful role models, guidance by mature and self-aware men who are not themselves infantilely enmeshed.

Hard Hat Area:
Destroying the Habitat of Soul

The dreamer in "The Men's Room" dream watches the owl fly past, feeling its every movement, as if for an instant he were the owl. As if now that he has been forced into such acute separateness, union with the owl—his sole or soul self—is all the more poignant, possible and necessary. For a moment he feels whole. Then the owl passes out of sight and hearing into the forest, and in the wave of a hand, the night has given way to morning. The daylight reveals a scene he didn't see when he arrived in the dark: all around the men's room sit huge yellow tractors, dump trucks, earth movers, and heavy machinery. Big green trees lie flattened all around, broken apart like matchsticks. Men in hard hats are clearing away the forest to make room for a parking lot. Everything feels meaningless again in the naked light of day. The owl is gone and he remembers his lover is gone, and instantaneously he feels empty and afraid: *no inner place to be.*

The hard hatted, self-alienated masculine—which he fears in himself, his father, and other men even as he has internalized it as a survival skill—has taken over again in the naked light of day and is destroying the only habitat he has been able to find for a less hostile, more soulful and receptive way of relating to himself. The hard hats are the aspect of himself that learned to get approval—or protect him from rejection—through performance and self-denial. This is the proper situation—or loss—for the dreamer to be grieving over, because he has spent much of his life as the hard hatted men destroying what would be a more receptive habitat for his deeper self or soul. Grieving over this loss is more crucial for him than the loss of his lover, which has served to cover up a much earlier and more profound loss of connection to himself in childhood.

The symbol in the dream of a man's relationship to himself and to other men—apart from woman, apart from feminine nurture—is of a barren, desolate, isolated men's room around which stands a forest that is home to an owl that unexpectedly brings comfort to the man. But the men, the workers, instead of making a place for this soulful relationship to themselves (the owl), are in the process of destroying its habitat. The men in hard hats are the part of the dreamer—and the aspect of masculine culture (which is not the exclusive domain of males) [2]—that has no room for a receptive relationship to itself, and thus to others and to nature.

This is why he is so depressed at the end of the dream: just when he finds some comfort for his pain, some sense of inner companionship, some place in himself that legitimizes and makes room for awareness, for his grief and

---

2. Gender roles are changing so rapidly now that it would be inaccurate to say that masculine culture as I describe it is necessarily the province of men more than women.

descent and the beginning of hope and transformation, the destructive side of the performing ego comes in with its heavy machinery, its extroverted get-the-job-done mentality and destroys the habitat of soul. Business as usual. This has been his experience of the masculine so far, and how he has internalized it as a way of relating to himself. No wonder the men's room at the back of his mind looks so forbidding, and continues to reinforce his precarious dependence on the outer feminine. As long as men are shamed for expressing the qualities our culture has designated and enforced as feminine—nurture, sensuality, compassion, playfulness—they will censor in themselves the same qualities they become desperately dependent on in women, the qualities that have been lost through the machinery of his socialization.

The dream also seems to be suggesting something about the fate of the earth if we continue to relate to it without awareness: we will destroy whatever we don't have a place for in our hearts and minds. When we lose touch with inner processes and how these are mirrored in nature, we no longer see ourselves and nature as interdependent.

Certain Australian Aboriginal tribes believe they must sing everything into existence or it will cease to be. They make a ritual journey—called a walkabout—through their tribal land during which they sing out every species of bird, tree, animal, and plant native to that part of the land, and this assures their continued existence. Songlines thus become psycho-spiritual-geographical boundaries made of song that protect and literally measure their world. The singing not only evokes awareness of these other life forms, it establishes a sympathetic connection with those life forms.

Living in nature they share the physical world with other animals and so feel a kinship, an affinity, a shared fate with the other animals of the earth which we in our air conditioned apartments and six-o-clock news world views no longer experience. So, as in the dream, we "pave paradise to put in a parking lot," as Joni Mitchell sings (and ironically, was singing over someone's radio as I wrote this paragraph). And who knows, maybe her songlines have helped save some pieces of paradise after all.

But they are no match for the iron Caterpillars tearing down the forest in the dream and on our planet, the machinery of a way of being that has lost touch with our deeper connection to self and earth.

In our urgency to expand markets and be successes, we destroy ecosystems and trample down the earth's species into extinction at a rate unprecedented in human history. By the year 2030 we will have destroyed half the earth's species and their habitats ("Silence of the Frogs"). These species are, at least symbolically, aspects of ourselves. Co-existence depends on our being able to appreciate life outside ourselves and being sensitive to others' needs. That assumes we are aware of and sensitive to our own.

We so easily trample ecosystems in the outer world because we do it so easily to ourselves on an inner level, perhaps as it was done to us unconsciously by others. All relationships begin with the one we have with ourselves. To the extent we are dehumanized, we do dehumanizing things. When we are pressured to clear-cut large sections of our psyche in order to fit into a family or be "productive members of society," we do this to nature without a second thought. The outer mirrors the inner. This is no secret. The forests are us.

4

Carrying Sleeping Moles

Denial, Repetition, and the Wounding into Awareness

Healing in dreams often takes the form of animals.
—Thomas Moore, *Care of the Soul*

The Dream

I'm leaving the house I once shared with my former girlfriend for five years, on my way to see my current girlfriend. I walk on the backyard path in the shade, carefully carrying a half dozen or more sleeping moles who hang trapped by their tails in large mousetraps. I don't want to touch them because they disgust me, so I carry them by holding the wooden flat of the traps. As I walk I feel an urgent need to keep the moles asleep and under control, afraid that if they get loose they'll keep me from getting to my girlfriend's house.

As we near a rock pile in the sunlight, the biggest mole begins to wake up. He writhes and twists violently, dangling from his tail in the metal crossbar of the trap. He is pinkish and hairy in places with a hairless underbelly. He looks fetus-like and is blind. I'm repulsed and don't want to touch him, but I put my hand over him firmly to try to calm and restrain him. He twists up violently and bites me hard on the finger, piercing my skin and drawing blood.

I've lost control of him, and now the other moles start to writhe around and wake up. I have to set them down on the rock pile to get a better hold on them, and as soon as I do the big mole gets loose from the trap and rumbles off slowly to hide in the rocks. As I chase him, the other moles squirm free and crawl off in all directions, disappearing into the rock pile. I race around to get them back under control, but I've lost them, and can't continue on to my girlfriend's.

*   *   *

The mole bite reminds us that whether we are in a relationship with someone else or not, we need to be in a conscious one with ourselves, and we ignore this at our peril.* This complex dilemma of looking for love is summed up poignantly by the twelfth century Persian poet, Jelaluddin Rumi:

> Lovers think they are looking for each other.

—"There's Nothing Ahead"

I dreamed "The Men's Room" dream at the painful end of a seven year relationship with a woman named Virginia. Four years later, at the beginning of my next long-term relationship, I dreamed about the moles. The house and backyard I'm trying to leave in the dream are where Virginia and I lived. Though it's been over five years since I had this dream, it has proven strangely prophetic. In a sense, I never did "reach my new girlfriend's house" in "real" life. Despite struggling for years to make our relationship work, it just brought out too many moles for each of us, so to speak, and we spent most of our time trying to get our "ugly" fears and projections under control. I see the image of "getting to my girlfriend's house" as symbolizing the desire to be loved, to reach the house of union and be able to participate fully in a loving relationship. Sometimes, it appears, our hearts need to be broken and handed back to us before we take enough responsibility for loving ourselves. Until then, getting to our lover's house becomes a precarious way of by-passing a relationship we need to first have with ourselves.

It is noteworthy that this dream at least partly originated from my reading of one of my key sources, Robert Bly's *Iron John*. The night I dreamed this dream, I had dinner with a friend and her cat named "Mousetrap." We discussed male dependence and the need to own one's issues, "crawl on one's belly." Before going to bed, I read in *Iron John* Bly's brief analysis of Hamlet's protracted wavering about avenging his father's murder. Bly reminds the reader that Hamlet's father's "mole voice" comes to him as if from underground, to remind him not to lose his purpose of avenging his murder by getting too caught up in his mother's infidelity. Hamlet is more worried about his mother's infidelity than his father's murder. The "mole voice" coming from his father is, according to Bly, a grounding or centering influence, the thing that would help him get unenmeshed from concerns about his mother so he could act as an individual, a man. His father comes to him in a mole voice to get him grounded in his masculine integrity at the point he is in danger of losing it in his attachment to mother, in his dependency on the external feminine.

Incidentally, the name of the play that Hamlet produces and refers to in the famous line, "The play's the thing/Wherein I'll catch the conscience of the king" (II, ii, 641), is also called "The Mousetrap." It appears that "the dream poet" in my head got the idea from my reading of Bly to put on a play of its own called "The Moletrap," with the same purpose of "catch[ing] the conscience of the king," that is, catching the part of me I keep trying to lose in my attachment to women but that would, if owned, ground me in the separateness and integrity associated with the king. One final note to shed light on the surprisingly intimate connection between my reading of *Iron John* and the dream content of "Carrying Sleeping Moles": I had just recently read a section of the book titled "Going from the Mother's House to Father's House" in which Bly remarks, "When initiation is in place, the old men help boys to move from the mother's world to the father's world" (86). Needless to say, in the dream I'm trying to get from one *girlfriend's house* to another. There is no house of the fathers, though in the previous dream there *is* a barren men's room.

In the dream, the moles stop the dreamer in front of the rock pile, which is the right place for him to stop, and at the right time...on his way into another relationship. The rock pile is an image of work still to be done. Not only is he stopped from proceeding unconsciously into another relationship by the rebellious moles, he must dig down and intentionally go after—*become conscious of*—these seemingly ugly estranged aspects of himself before he can get to his girlfriend's house, before he can go into another relationship without holding someone else hostage to what he is estranged from in himself—a situation which is mirrored by his keeping the moles in traps.

Much as he'd like to, he can't just set the moles down and proceed to his girlfriend's without them because they represent the least conscious and most rejected depths of himself, which we all need and involuntarily encounter in any intimate relationship. We can't get to the loving relationship we want with someone else until we begin a more conscious and accepting one with ourselves. So the dream intervenes to turn the dreamer's attention from his girlfriend to the moles and the rock pile where he now must bring into awareness—into the sunlight—the psychological content he's tried to deny or even unload in a relationship to someone else.

What we consider as the defective aspects of our personality often lead us to the deepest parts of ourselves. But because we have been denying or burying them since they met with disapproval in childhood, we are either completely unconscious of them or they appear to us now as monstrously ugly: pinkish, fetus-like, hairy with hairless underbellies, blind and unpredictable—things we don't want to associate with ourselves. The dream ego doesn't even want to touch them, especially now that he's on his way to see his girlfriend, and so he carries them by the wooden traps they dangle upside down from by their tails. He would disown them if he could, but since they symbolize aspects of himself, the psyche won't let him go on without them.

The more we refuse to relate to these rejected parts of ourselves, the more fearful and ugly they become, and the more twisted become their attempts to penetrate our consciousness. Jung tells us that everything in the unconscious seeks to manifest itself in consciousness, seeks to be integrated into the self. And where we resist unconscious content, it manifests itself in distorted ways, through anxiety, through our projections onto others, and through our dreams where we at least have the opportunity to own what we have tried to disown.

He's "in a hurry" to get away from his last relationship, and in a hurry to get to his girlfriend's, and so the moles slow him down and stop him from *getting elsewhere*. *The bite wounds him into the more conscious relationship he needs to have with himself.*

It is also significant that the action occurs in the shade in the back yard of his previous relationship, which suggests unfinished business. We take to our next relationship all that remains asleep or unconscious in us, all we that push underground and refuse to relate to, i.e. all our psychological baggage.

The dream suggests that this time, however, as the dreamer starts getting deeper into another relationship, he is ready for his moles to awaken. The dream ego is resistant and even opposed to the moles waking up, but the unconscious content in the form of the trapped moles can't be contained any longer in a repressed state. The awakening of the moles is a frightening and disorienting ordeal that we usually try to avoid, even if it means leaving the person who has awoken our moles, i.e. started "pushing our buttons" and bringing out our intimacy fears and wounds. Without the proper psychological tools for dealing with these newly awakened fears, many find it necessary to leave the relationship and avoid situations of intimacy rather than be confronted with their seemingly uncontrollable, "ugly" shadow side.

A culture so preoccupied with image and success puts a lot of pressure on all of us to show up in relationships without any problems—*mole-free*, so to speak. But, of course, dealing with our mole aspects has to be part of the process of being in a relationship, especially—the dream reminds us—the relationship to ourselves.

When we begin to take into account our mole aspects, the quest for love and intimacy shifts from looking for it exclusively in someone else to looking for it through a process of self-awareness and relatedness. We become an observer of ourselves, which creates enough inner space for insight and growth. We cease pushing away and being ashamed of difficult parts of ourselves, and this enables us to be more present with others as well, less externalized and judgmental. But as long as we aren't inhabiting our mole regions, we by-pass this relationship to ourselves and unconsciously try to get others to take care of it. This locates our center precariously outside ourselves in someone else, who we then feel compelled to possess and control—trap—for our well being, security or self-esteem, an unstable situation that often leads to much grief and sometimes violence.

Until we start to relate to what we regard as these disgusting mole aspects, we externalize, i.e. project unconsciously onto others, what should be part of a conscious relationship to ourselves. And to the extent we begin to accept our mole aspects, we are freed from spending so much energy trying to keep them trapped and asleep.

Once again the movement in the dream is downwards, this time into the image of the underground dwelling moles—perhaps a dream strategy to counter a culture and the dreamer's tendency to be overly concerned with looking good on the surface. The image of the trap symbolizes the censorship the dream ego attempts over his dark side or banished self he is unconsciously ashamed of and unreceptive to. What we deny returns again and again. Denial leads to repetition, a function or phenomenon of the psyche Freud called "the return of the repressed."

In this case, the repressed content finds its way into a dream in which it, in the form of the trapped mole, finally bites the dream ego, piercing his skin and shedding blood. In the economy of the psyche, it wants to be related to. Fear and defensiveness lead to rigid ego boundaries, stopping the flow and leading to contraction, dis-ease. Repression is not efficient: In *Care of the Soul*, Thomas Moore observes that mental illness occurs wherever there is a lack of "imagination," a lack of movement or choices. It is noteworthy that the mole bites the dream ego only after he refuses to free the mole from the trap, and tries to restrain it and keep it asleep.

The Trance of Denial and Repetition

The dreamer in "Carrying Sleeping Moles" feels he needs to hurry while at the same time keeping these disgusting little ugly mole aspects trapped and asleep, under control. He doesn't know how to relate to these aspects of himself except repressively. He doesn't have time for this sort of problem, especially since he's in a rush to get to someone whose attention he is coming to depend on increasingly more than his own for his sense of self-worth and security—which is another reason the mole bites him: to get his attention and wake him up from the trap **he** is in, the trap of having to go to someone else for a more loving relationship to himself.

The moles trap *us* when we try to control them so they won't upset the image or personality we think will be more liked or loved by others. Denial and defensiveness prevent us from becoming conscious of these unconscious constellated identities, so they could evolve. As it is, these rejected mole identities remain in a primitive, infantile state, what Steven Wolinsky calls "trances." Trances or unconscious identities are the unconscious strategies we adopt in order to survive—physically and emotionally—traumatic childhood situations over which we had no control. These are our oldest most primitive coping mechanisms, mechanisms which, when unconscious, continue to create the situation they defended us from in the first place. The primitivism of these aspects of self is reflected in the image of the mole, one of the most primitive of all mammals.

The Mole Latitudes

We all carry around sleeping mole aspects of ourselves that we think are defective and ugly and we don't want to touch, and that we hope will never wake up, especially when we're on our way to our lover's house. But it's precisely because we are on our way to see our lover that the moles have surfaced. Sooner or later, the landscape of intimacy brings out our infantile or repressed fears and feelings about ourselves. These are the feelings we haven't dealt with consciously and that come out the closer we get to someone else because this intimate proximity replicates our original relationship with the parents and all the often unconscious assumptions about ourselves and others that this brings up: feelings of worth and worthlessness, confidence and inadequacy, abandonment and security, lovableness and unlovableness, feelings and beliefs that, when unconscious, drive us into false or compensating personas *and relationships.*

The trouble is when we avoid the moles, we lose touch with our depths. *This is when we are more prepared for what we fear than for what we want.*

When we can't allow ourselves to become conscious of these core messages about ourselves—however inaccurate they really are—they never change, never evolve out of the infancy or primitivism of our experience of them. Avoiding these, we go everywhere in life but inside ourselves where our true center of balance and power is, where we know what we want and don't want, where we buried our king or queen in childhood. Intimacy means *innermost*; when we are trying to conceal our innermost expectations of ourselves from others, we get cut off from the innermost in ourselves, and become self-alienated.

We would prefer that these ugly feelings stay underground, as is the custom of moles, who tunnel, burrow, and feed on roots and insects and the worms that fall into their extensive tunnel systems, enabling them to almost never have to come above ground in plain sight, where they are extremely clumsy and vulnerable…much like the aspects of ourselves we reject.

The moles become the emblem of our fear and self-rejection, not an accurate representation of who we really are. They contain the judgments and reactions of others who we were often dependent upon for our survival and who we then internalized as a way of relating to ourselves. The "ugly" moles represent what we then rejected in ourselves, which is why they are so valuable to us now as a compass to recovering the disowned self.

An important principle here is that this shaming and censorship occur on both a familial and cultural level. The mole aspects we feel compelled to repress are different for each person; what is perhaps more universal is that in masculine culture there is pressure to banish those aspects of the self that interfere with fulfilling the three P's: provide. perform, protect, which spell a fourth, pathology, when not balanced by other more nurturing and receptive modes of being. In traditional masculine culture, a man learns to deny anything that raised questions about his ability to "get the job done" or keep in control, compete with other men—needs, fears, feelings of failure, inadequacy, weakness, feeling hurt, sad, lonely. This is usually the ground on which men have been most shamed in their lives, and consequently where they buried their most intuitive self or inner child.

One example of how we as a culture create these mole aspects through shaming concerns a man's sexuality, which is immediately turned into a performance when we call it his "virility." When he doesn't sustain an erection—or "get it up"—we call it "impotence," a word laden with the judgment that something is wrong with him, defective, not potent. We do the same thing to a woman when she doesn't orgasm or enjoy sex, and we call her "frigid." It is that much more an issue for the man, since he can't hide his "symptoms." These terms ("impotence" and "frigidity") reveal our unreceptiveness to our bodies' messages, to psychological events, while reinforcing the emphasis on physical or external outcomes, rather than inner processes.

Love and Moles

In an almost comic attempt to conceal his "defects," the dream ego heads to his lover's house literally wearing the trapped moles on his sleeve, hoping not to wake them. *As if we could conceal these parts of ourselves in a relationship of any depth!* Once we get to the depths with anyone, we run into our mole aspects. This is one of the great yet unwelcome opportunities of love. *It seems to be one of the unconscious goals of love to bring us into relationship with another person in such a way that asks us to relate to more of ourselves.* We grow up assuming that these mole aspects are negative, defective and undesirable, and will lead others to reject us. We then create more heroic, unblemished alternative personalities, hoping to win love and attention, like a dog doing tricks, standing on its hind legs for the reward of a bone. Sooner or later we discover the opportunity to settle back more comfortably onto all fours, so to speak, and go on with life better grounded in ourselves. The dream represents a less comfortable, preliminary stage of this process.

When we are not in a relationship, we are often better able to avoid and be detached from these rejected aspects of ourselves, and free to fantasize about the perfect lover and the idealized self. We often seek to be loved in those places we have most abandoned ourselves, so that our "ideal" lover fits perfectly the shape of our inner emptiness. But take one step closer to someone or dig down a little deeper, asking to be loved, and these creatures of our primordial self-image emerge, reminders of whatever landscape of love and fear, rejection or nurture we experienced in the infancy of our personality.

When in childhood we unconsciously reject the parts of ourselves that others disapproved of or didn't support, and instead develop personalities that better satisfy the needs of others whose love and approval we needed, we get committed to being who we aren't; we get committed to personalities that don't express our deepest needs.

If we can begin to love our mole selves, we are increasingly able to inhabit our neglected depths and less likely to try to inhabit someone else's or to base our self-worth solely in external situations. The moles are another manifestation of the men's room, and both are symbols of the barren inner landscape that the dreamer's dreams are asking him to relate to consciously in order to transform, and which he has tried to by-pass in his relationships with women. To quote the poet Emily Dickinson, a bit of an a-social mole herself:

> Reverse cannot befall
> that fine prosperity
> whose sources are interior.

—(188; #395)

This is mole wisdom.

The Wounding into Awareness: Relativizing the Ego

The reason the moles seem so ugly and disgusting is that they mirror the dreamer's attitude about parts of himself he's rejecting, on the level of ego. Getting to the point where we accept ourselves without grandiose, compensating personas always involves going into the wounds that we covered up with these compensations in the first place. So it involves a struggle with the ego, that part of us constellated to defend ourselves against hurt and ambiguity.

The ego makes sure we survive, and to this end seeks definition, control, and reduction of ambiguity in our relation both to the outside world and to our inner selves. The more we become conscious and receptive, the less rigid and defensive the ego needs to be, because by facing our latent fears, we defuse the need for ego defenses that arose in childhood to protect us from perceived danger or injury. Yet as long as we avoid the vicinity of our wounds we go on fearing the same outcome, preparing for it and thereby helping to bring it about, whether we're talking about being betrayed, abandoned, rejected or failing at things.

The dream enables the dreamer to observe his ego self with detachment. Hence, the dream relativizes the ego to other aspects of self, while the dreamer or "observing ego" looks on.

The mole aspects want to be related to, even if it means penetrating the ego's denial with a violent bite. *The mole bite represents the wounding by which the dream wounds the dreamer into a deeper awareness of himself, which he has been resisting. To be bitten is to be penetrated, initiated.* This is consistent with countless ritual practices in which wounding, scarification, and physical ordeals are the means by which a tribe or community wakes up the initiate into a more acute awareness of responsibility (response ability) and inner resources.

The bite relativizes the ego to these unconscious aspects we've been denying. This is what gives us depth, texture, resonance, compassion and imagination as human beings. Relativizing the ego is especially important for men who have been socialized to rigidify ego boundaries in order to compete against each other, perform, focus on goals and outcomes—sometimes on the battlefield where to lose is to die, sometimes on the playground or in business or in the bedroom where to lose is to be shamed. The focus on outer measures, goals and trophies leads to a self-alienation that the mole bite interrupts. Even though it comes in a dream, the imagery offers medicine on a symbolic level—*to be taken internally.*

The bite that draws blood is a serious matter for the dreamer; it means he is ready to confront some deeper, core issues without losing track of them in a relationship to someone else, in this case, once again, to the external feminine. The bite can also be seen as symbolizing the blood-letting or skin piercing that often accompanies initiation rituals. There is much resistance on the dream ego's part, so, on the level of the psyche, the wounding has to hurt enough to penetrate his defenses, yet not so much that it only makes him more defensive, commits him to more denial or a retrenching in the ego.

Part of what needs to happen during these woundings and descents is the death of our ego defenses which are preventing us from achieving a more conscious and expansive relationship to ourselves. This doesn't mean our ego must die and disappear, just that it must die in the sense of transformation and growth. Rilke darkly celebrates a form of transformation in the following lines quoted earlier from his *Duino Elegies*:

For beauty is nothing but the beginning of terror
That we're still just able to bear.
And the reason we love it so
Is because it serenely disdains to destroy us.

Hegel refers to the death of the ego as a necessary estrangement from the self, that territory where familiar self meets hitherto unknown possibilities of being. It seems that we go on forming and shedding such boundaries of the self and ego defenses all our lives; these are as necessary to our survival as the outer skin is to a piece of fruit: it must be pliant in order to be able to expand.

If we can't cultivate a place inside ourselves for soul, we may go to someone else in a regressive search for security in the form of *his* or *her* emotional womb. This outer quest for inner peace is often the fate of those of us who learned in childhood we had to perform to get attention; we had to *go out of ourselves* to seek the approval of others, and were thus taught to distrust the more authentic self. *When we succeed at getting someone else to take care of our mole aspects, we institutionalize our self-alienation through a relationship or marriage.* This is the stuff that co-dependence and power struggles are made of.

The bite on the finger wakes up the dreamer to the need to be grounded in himself. *The wound must get through his defenses without leaving him defenseless, and the dream mechanism seems mysteriously adept at gauging these measured woundings into awareness. The moles are the part of us that make sure we get to our own house before we make it to someone else's.*

The Mole as Mentor to The Man

As in the Men's Room dream, the dream asks the dreamer to make a descent into himself to find some reliable ground, rather than looking for it in someone else. And something about the moles makes them the right animal for the job.

Being virtually blind, as well as one of the most primitive and, arguably "ugliest" animals, the mole seems a fitting symbolic antidote to a culture and a dreamer obsessed with images and appearances of skin deep beauty and success. The mole is the perfect mascot for the descent the man is being asked to make; its foreclaws are evolved more than any other animal for digging underground, where it spends nearly all its life, tunneling, living on insects and roots, blind to the distractions of the visual, surface world. Because moles are either blind or live underground in total darkness, they are not distracted by the visual world the way humans are; they are therefore very intimate with their other senses, the feeling sensors all over the body, the sense of touch and smell and hearing—senses that have atrophied in humans as we have increased our reliance on intellect and technology. Moles rely on their senses to be intimate with the landscape in ways that those of us who are not blind can only imagine. The mole doesn't get lost in abstractions or visual distractions. *Unlike us, it cannot intellectualize itself so much that it loses touch with its body, its senses of smell, hearing, and touch, or it will lose touch with the landscape and die.* We are no longer intimate with the landscape we nonetheless depend on. We get dissociated from our bodies when we become imbalanced by the injunctions to be assertive and stoic, and then dissociated from nature and habitat.

The mole tells us that to become dissociated from our bodies, obsessed with goals and abstract futures is to become dissociated from a part of ourselves that is grounded in our bodies, in the landscape, in the sensuous world, a part of us that is self-reliant. When the father is not physically and emotionally present for the son, the son gets cut off from these depths in himself—from his own body, from a corporeal sense of security and integrity—and is more likely to become *dependent*, as in infancy and childhood, on a woman's body for his sense of physical well being.

To be dissociated from our bodies—lacking a sensual receptivity and relatedness to them and thus to the landscape and to others—is to be left urgently dependent, as when we were infants, on a woman's body. Perhaps this is another reason the dreamer is in such a rush in the dream to get to his girlfriend's house. For men, the lack of a sensual relationship to themselves can so easily keep them trapped in dependence on the female and her physical body. As James Hollis writes,

> Sexuality, in particular, is freighted with the infantile need for bodily contact and nurturance. As women grow weary of taking care of little boys, so little boys find it harder and harder to leave home and grow up, since neither father nor the fathers are available to show the way (35).

If we accept the idea from Thomas Moore in *Care of the Soul* that the "healing in dreams often takes the form of animals," we can see the moles as interrupting the dreamer from a regressive infantile move back to mother—in the form of the girlfriend he's desperate to reach—to get him to stop and relate to his wounded, neglected masculine integrity. Since the fathers weren't there to guide him into this ground in himself, thus balancing out the identification of his physical and emotional survival with mother, the dream provides a necessary intervention.

The further we have gotten into the injunction to be above all a performer, and the further we become entrenched in the paraphernalia of this dictum—the metropolitan-industrial landscape ruled by technology, computers, machines, clocks and deadlines, concrete, asphalt, freeways, cars, competition, efficiency and the future—the less we have opportunities to listen to our bodies and live sensuously, and the more our senses have atrophied. The less we experience consciousness through our body sensorium, the less we live sensuously in the immediate physical world or the immediate moment. This leads to having less connectedness to and awareness of habitat, a point that was crucial in the Men's Room dream, since what we don't have room for in awareness we neglect and often destroy—both on an inner and outer level. The loss of a natural habitat impoverishes our animal body, and we in turn impoverish or destroy our natural habitat.

The moles are trapped by their *tails* in the large mousetraps, much like we are trapped by our *tales*—which is all that is behind us—when we remain asleep, unconscious. Our tails/tales are the most primitive part of us, our history and family drama, our unconscious selves, and we have to come to terms with them consciously if we are ever to be freed from the trap of repeating the past. As long as the dreamer goes from one house of relationship to another without getting grounded in himself, his integrity as an individual is in a trap. If he doesn't begin to get grounded in himself he will never get to his girlfriend's house on the right footing for a healthy relationship.

Our inability to descend to and accept these rejected, shadow aspects finally gets in the way of our expressing happiness, spontaneity, joy and intimacy. How can we move with any lightness or love or intuitive grace if we're carrying around so much of ourselves in traps? We hang in traps by our tails—all that is behind us in our past and childhood which we haven't put in front of us in the light of consciousness. The mole bite stops the dreamer from repeating his cycle of denial and provides the necessary wounding into the awareness of how his integrity as a self is in a trap as long as he's avoiding his shadow self in his romantic relationships.

5

The Shaman in the Disco

Initiation into the Deeper Self

The shaman in traditional societies was the healer, the one who restored life, who found lost souls, and who discovered the hidden causes of misfortune. He was the one who restored wholeness and fullness of being to individuals and communities.... Often, in difficult situations...people are drawn into some kind of space and time frame that can be called "sacred"...This "sacred" space is something that men who are guided by the [Shaman] know very well. These men may actually put themselves into that space deliberately...

—(Moore and Gillette, Magician Within 110)

The Dream

I've been away on a long and difficult train trip to get closer to my father, but it didn't work out the way I'd hoped. I return home feeling depressed, homeless and out of sorts. Instead of going home to my apartment I go to my girlfriend's. She's been busy working all day and now she wants to go out on the town drinking and dancing. I sit on her bed, desperately needing to talk to her. I want her to sit down on the bed and listen to me, but the harder I try to get her to sit down, the more oblivious she is to me. I keep trying to talk to her, but she just rushes around the room in a mini-skirt, laughing and talking non-stop—which only doubles my estrangement.

As she rushes around I notice she has a third eye, right above the bridge of her nose. It's small, like a mole's eye, and I wonder if she can see with it. It strikes me that, even though she has this remarkable third eye, she just sees more distractions with it.

The scene shifts and I'm at a basement level dance club or disco. A numbingly repetitious bass beat reverberates through the dark, cavernous club. Big thick bass notes repeat the pattern over and over again: dum-dum, dum-dum-dum, dum-dum, dum-dum, dum-dum, dum-dum-dum. It's as if I'm seeing this all through a movie camera; it shows a close-up of a man's sport coat clad shoulder jerking mechanically to the beat. The camera-like perspective slowly moves up the sleeve of what appears to be a huge muscular arm and shoulder. I'm in awe at first at the size of the man, until the camera backs off to a wider angle and shows that his head is the size of a fist, and it becomes clear the shoulders of his sport coat have been grotesquely over-padded. I see that the disco is filled with young fraternity boys in glittery gold sport coats that exaggerate the size of their shoulders, making their fist-sized heads look even smaller. They all move mechanically, as if robots connected to the beat by gears.

A glittering mirror ball hangs from the ceiling, revolving around in the center of the disco, throwing fragments of light on the robotic dancers. I stand there depressed and alienated, mocking the beat and the movements of the frat boys, who seem like unconscious automatons. Just then an older black man sitting on the floor of a raised platform in the middle of the club motions me over to him. He drifts contentedly on the rhythmic beat and looks like he's drunk or strung out on something. This disappoints and irritates me, so I ignore him. But he calls out to me, "Come here," as if he knows what I'm feeling, and immediately gets my attention. As I walk toward him, he smiles all glassy eyed and I realize he's tripping on drugs. I feel let down, and motion him away with my hands so he'll leave me alone.

He calls to me again in a languorous drugged voice, "Hey man, come over here." I gesture emphatically for him to leave me alone, becoming more impatient and angry with his intrusions. Suddenly, with the urgency and authority of someone pounding a table, he tells me, "Come here now!" He looks me straight in the eyes, focused and unflinching, and I feel his penetrating gaze go right inside me. Without hesitation, I walk over to him. By the time I cross the disco floor, he seems to have reverted to his stupor, and I become bitter yet again that he has let me down. His movements are slow and loose, his eyes glazed over and watery. He smiles a slow wide open smile, and says, "Man, I know what you're going through." I become indignant that he's cheapening my pain, and I say coldly, "I really doubt it," and start to walk away. But just then, he immediately sobers up, looks me piercingly in the eyes and says with an authority that goes right into me, "I know exactly what you're going through."

His eyes lock onto mine and everything slows down. Time seems to stand still. The noise and crowd of the disco that surrounded us a moment before, have fallen away into a distant world. We are in a different reality, slow, focused, clear. The panic I felt ever since trying to connect with my girlfriend instantly subsides, and I feel focused and calm. He remains staring straight into my eyes, and I feel comforted deep down inside. As he stands in front of me. I realize he's not wearing a shirt anymore, or the rest of his clothes. Around his neck hang ceremonial beads, and bones or sticks. His face is smudged with ashes and white mud. He lifts his right hand into the air and spreads his fingers outwards in what seems a ritual movement, then extends his hand toward me and places it on my heart. There is an electric shock like a cattle prod or lightning bolt of darkness and I am instantly taken from my mind into a dark cave-like reality with him, the cave of myself, deep within my body, where I've never been before. I feel a deep sense of security and well being.

Everything here is distilled to its essential primitive reality. Fires burn away all that is false or extraneous. Only the truth survives. For the first time I feel entirely focussed, at peace and centered. There are no distractions and I feel no fear. We stay here a while in the darkness and torch light. Then I see the shaman's hand pulling back from my chest and we're back outside my body, separate again. He stands in front of me in full ritual dress: he wears a grass matt skirt and crown like hat, and holds a wooden staff in one hand. A fire burns slowly in front of us and there is a sound of faint drumming.

With his eyes fixed on mine, the shaman lifts up his hand and looks at me as if to say, "Watch closely; I am going to show you what you need to know." Two finger sized spears sprout up like twigs from his hand where his fingers would normally be. Their shafts are wrapped in red and white ribbon. Showing the first pair of spears, he shakes his head as if to say, "This is not the way inside yourself." And then another pair of spears sprouts up next to the other pair, and he shakes his head again as if to say, "This is not the way inside yourself," Finally, a fifth spear emerges where his thumb would otherwise be, separate and singular from the other spears, and he looks at me as if to say, "This is your answer." I look at him confused and say out loud, "But I don't know what it means." He looks at me and says without words, "You will."

*   *   *

The dream of "The Shaman in the Disco" returns to the archetypal situation of the man looking for his soul in his relationship to a woman. In the dream, he is at a loss to know why he feels so desperately self-alienated. He does what he learned to do, what his culture even advertises as a cure for problems of the soul: he looks for someone or something outside to fill the void inside—the perfect career or the perfect lover. Unprepared to befriend these darker states of the soul, we look everywhere but inside to heal our pain and this only leads us further from ourselves. Hence, just as in the dream when he seeks rescue from the three-eyed woman, his fear and soul loss increase, and a subdued panic sets in.

The train trip to see his father and establish the bond that has been lacking between them all his life becomes a microcosmic re-enactment of his child-hood experience of his father as unavailable and disapproving, and he comes back home depressed, alienated from his father and consequently from him-self. In fact, I dreamed this dream the night I returned home from a train trip to visit my father feeling estranged, as usual, from both him and myself. But instead of going home to my house, I went to my girlfriend's to get her to make me feel better. It was a move I have made repeatedly in all my romantic relationships, and a move the dream ego tries to make in the mole dream. But the dream would not let me by-pass this inner estrangement, and instead looked for a way to get me to own and transform it.

The father wound is ultimately a wound to one's self-image. Disconnected from his father, he has been unable to father himself. Going to his three-eyed externalized lover only makes his inner estrangement worse. The attempt to lose one's self-alienation in attachments to other is doomed to backfire. It's not until the unlikely guide in the disco looks him right in the eye and says, "I know exactly what you're going through," that he experiences, at least symbol-ically, a version of the soul healing or attentive fathering he has wanted all his life—so he can internalize it as a way of relating to himself.

Self-Alienation and the Three-Eyed Woman

The soul is not just some warm sentiment that we carry around with us to be taken out at need and otherwise ignored.
She, too, requires relatedness—to one's inner world. She, too, requires something of a man's time and effort.

—(Johnson, *We* 79)

Characterized as she is by an outward seeing third eye, the three-eyed woman becomes the image of his externalized search for centeredness and soul, a search which inevitably becomes more panicked and self-alienating the more it is directed outwards. The dreamer has proceeded through these dreams by a succession of failed attempts to find his sense of "home" outside himself, through others, until, finally, hopeless and at a total loss for what to do, the shaman appears and turns his attention inward where it needs to be so that he can internalize the fathering as a way of taking care of himself—a process more appropriate to childhood but postponed when the father is absent, negating or otherwise unreliable.

Not knowing how to be with his inner alienation he brings it to his girlfriend and experiences it, inaccurately, as estrangement between them. This perilous move to seek one's psychological moorings in someone else is to a great extent the fulfillment of our cultural fantasy of "love." But it is even more perilous for a man when he tries to replace the nurturing relationship he needs to have with himself, by a relationship to a woman. Doing this just reinforces his infantile dependence and rage when his lover doesn't act the role of the nurturing mother. Hollis elaborates,

> All the neediness of their inner child remains active in the present, as well as his fear of the mother's power to overwhelm or abandon him. This is why so many men seek to control their partner, for they feel the Other, as before, is all powerful still…(59).

That this attempt is doomed is made abundantly clear when the girlfriend he tries to connect with has a third eye which serves only to make her more distracted and extroverted—a symbol of his lack of a conscious relationship with his own inner life or inner "feminine." The mini-skirt is also an emblem of externalization, to the extent it signifies how women can become self-alienated in our culture when they seek affirmation primarily through getting attention as sex objects. The mini-skirt also symbolizes male externalization in the form of men as "skirt chasers".

When his attempt to bond with his three-eyed girlfriend fails, the dreamer feels doubly hopeless and isolated, seemingly with nowhere to turn—not even to himself. Externalizing the relationship we need to have with ourselves is always a desperate undertaking. Internalizing it is difficult as well, and the need to do so evokes the dream itself and the shaman image.

The descent into ourselves leads us to solid ground and psychological gravity so that we're not suffering the fate of the "unbearable lightness of being"—that Kunderean realm of pure possibility—avoiding our shadow selves, our histories, and the intimacy with another that requires an intimacy with the self. Without such grounding in ourselves, we get stuck in adolescence, the Peter Pan puer figure who keeps flying away to never never land, and thus never grows up.

The three-eyed woman is the aspect of the dreamer that is focussed on the outside world at a cost of a deeper relationship to his soul depths; she represents his externalized search for soul and for a more sensual, nurturing relationship to himself, his body, senses, time.

As we have already seen, men frequently put a woman's body between themselves and their experience of physical pleasure and well being, in accordance with our socialization. Her body was there, after all, before and while we were emerging into the world. From our earliest experience in the mother's womb we come to identify not only our nurture and pleasure, but our very material being and survival with the outer feminine. Hollis offers a compelling explanation for this sort of male dependency that would otherwise be balanced out by a nurturing father. It bears quoting at length:

> I have seen a considerable number of men whose need for mothering is so extensive that they are doomed to be dissatisfied with their wives. While it is clear that women do not want to be mothers to their husbands, it is also clear that many men seek in their wives the sort of unconditional acceptance and nourishment associated with positive mothers. Indeed, I have seen many men stuck in marriages that were dreadful for various reasons, but they were unable to countenance the idea of leaving. Departure held all the terrors of the child leaving home for the unknown. Sexuality, in particular, is freighted with the infantile need for bodily contact and nurturance. As women grow weary of taking care of little boys, so little boys find it harder and harder to leave home and grow up, since neither father nor the fathers are available to show the way (35)....

> Jungian analyst Guy Corneau points out that men grow alienated from their own bodies as well, for they associate their corporeal reality with the early, primal contact with the mother. As they were seldom hugged or held by their fathers, they correlate matter with mother, and disconnect from their bodies" (37)....

It is not hard to see why adult intimate relationships are troubled, given the primacy of the mother encounter. All our unassimilated need, fear and rage are acted out in intimate relationships (59)…. Sexual intimacy is especially freighted with this archaic burden, because having sex is for many men the primal reconnection, the closest they ever feel to the positive mother (60).

When we've lacked the presence of a nurturing father, we identify our own pleasure and well being more with the female body than with our own, which bespeaks serious self-alienation. The three-eyed woman signifies that the dreamer has projected onto a woman the relationship he needs to have with himself.[1]

In Hindu religion, the third eye represents the sixth chakra, vision, the spiritual, or inward-seeing eye that makes a place for soul in our lives. *That her third eye in the dream is solely an outward seeing eye suggests the absence of this inward spiritual self-awareness or connection in the dreamer.* Focusing on or

---

1. In a nutshell, the following factors underlie the correlation between male self-alienation and the dependence on woman as sensual sexual object:

    (1) We evolve into physical form in the mother's body.

    (2) Most of our physical contact and nurture have traditionally come from the mother. In the absence of a nurturing father, we are totally dependent on her for survival; we learn about love and attachment from whatever she has to give (or not give), and this determines our image of the love object we will thereafter unconsciously seek in love. On an unconscious level, we equate her body with our material and emotional well being.

    (3)Being socialized as performers and competitors (produce, provide, protect) has encouraged us to subordinate our bodies and minds to goals and work, leading us often into a hostile, and precluding a more sensual, relationship to our bodies, ourselves.

    (4) The pervasive objectification-eroticization of the female body, female image or mystique in television, advertising, film, fashion and literature feeds men's obsession with fantasy projections of women as sexual, nurture objects which play on men's unconscious infantile dependence and desensualized relationship to their own bodies, reinforcing both men's and women's alienation from self and each other, i.e. she as sex object, he as success object.

becoming obsessed with the seductive or externalized woman who doesn't listen to us is part of the dreamer's infantile heritage he needs to wake up from. What he really needs is to connect with a part of *himself* that will listen. Looking for a relationship with someone else that will enable him to by-pass the unconscious and wounded one he has with himself no longer works.

The three-eyed woman symbolizes how we all, to some degree, externalize in love a relationship we need to make more conscious with ourselves. For women, the precariousness often comes when they become dependent on men for things they have been conditioned to repress in themselves: assertiveness, stoicism, professional ambition, financial security. It has traditionally been along these lines that she would be apt to objectify and control a man—culturally sponsored gender repression that leads, in both men and women, to a form of emotional hostage-taking.

The dreamer attempts to connect with someone who has no interest or ability for such engagement. At his level of self-estrangement he is unable to judge the compatibility of other people with his deeper wants and needs, and, moreover, is capable of doing the most desperate things as long as the relationship to his inner feminine has been externalized in someone else. (True intimacy involves accepting the other as separate from our needs. This means we can't abandon being conscious of ourselves in an intoxicated merger with our fantasy projection.)

The Disco of Denial
and Meeting the Guide

When a man consents to begin the interior journey, the symbolic quest...a guide or teacher is of inestimable aid...Going into the depths indicates that the experience is profoundly inward and solitary...

—(Johnson, *Transformation* 76-77)

When you start on a quest, you may not have the slightest idea of what you're looking for. You are looking for the Magician [Shaman]. But the goal being sought isn't out there in the world, it is deep inside. And one of the purposes of initiation is to teach that simple truth.

—(Moore and Gillette, *Magician Within* 80)

In the disco, the dream ego unconsciously seeks help, some form of intervention that he has been unable to provide for himself up to this point in his life. He is ready to move to a deeper level of consciousness, but because he lacks the knowledge of even the process, he loiters about the disco at a loss.

Even when help or mentoring is available, we're not always receptive to it. Our experience of the father as either critical or supportive will shape our expectations of and receptivity to mentoring, and by extension, to community. The critical or negating father leads sons to mistrust men, especially when they need them most. Such a son will be wary of seeking any sort of help, advice or apprenticeship, and suffer in the safety of the isolation or anger he escaped to in childhood. The healthy individual knows when and how to ask for help, based on positive experience in childhood, and knows that this is in no way a diminishment of self, while individuals who need it most have become progressively least able to ask.

So, one of the problems for a young man when he experiences an unavailable or negating father is that he gives up on male guides and mentors; he doesn't expect them and he doesn't look for them. He also stops trusting the father and gives up hope for the masculine. As Bly says in *Iron John*, the son grows up thinking that he has reached manhood if he only rejects his father. He has become like a plant that has endured a long drought by withering into a tiny knot of survival—a desert cactus. No buds, no flowers. In this form one survives rather than lives, expecting and thus preparing for scarcity instead of abundance, criticism or competition instead of support or understanding, violence—economic and otherwise—instead of compassion. And armoring himself against this anticipated antagonism, he helps create it.

What we are experiencing today in the worst case of the absent father and the absence of adequate initiators, are gangs of young boy-men trapped in violent ritualistic ways of proving a masculine identity they are frightfully unsure about, while facing a future even less promising. Gang membership in Los Angeles alone swelled to over 70,000 in the 1990's. The fraternity boys in the dream wearing exaggerated suits are a less extreme version of the gang members who've been abandoned by their fathers, and whose compensatory shows of bravado are often fatal. For the most at risk group of males, black men between the ages of sixteen and twenty-four, murder is the leading cause of death (*Myth of Male Power* 30, 181). A broader consequence is an increase in violence to women; when his mother dependency is not mitigated by the presence of the father, he takes the insecurity to women, increasing his dependence on, resentment of and compulsion to control her.

One of the most haunting examples of fatherless boys in modern literature is William Golding's unsettling novel, *Lord of the Flies*, about what happens to a shipwrecked group of British school boys when they are marooned on an island without any older men to help structure their fear and energy. In the absence of older men, they turn their escalating fear into outward acts of ferocity and violence against each other, culminating in the more aggressive boys hunting down and killing the less aggressive boys. A similar fate has awaited an increasing number of fatherless boys marooned on the island of adolescence, a hostile economy, and in many minority communities.

The father, older man, uncle, or mentor must be able to contain the young man's fears, rages, hopes and frustrations without taking them personally, becoming resentful or competitive. This means he must know himself, his inner landscape, be able to provide for his own inner needs so he can nurture others. This ability is what enables a parent to parent and to focus on the child's needs without projecting his own unresolved issues onto his children. When the parents' experience has cut them off from vital psychological information about themselves, their ability to understand or even acknowledge their children's needs, much less provide for them and guide them, is severely compromised.

Luke Skywalker

The most popular adventure-initiation film of our time—the *Star Wars* trilogy—resonates with its audience partly because of the issues we are concerned with here: the hole left by the absent father and the profound need young men have for elder males to help initiate them into their psychological depths. At the outset of the trilogy, we are introduced to Luke Skywalker, a young man who has never known his father. He has been raised by an unhappy uncle who is more interested in what Luke can do for him on the farm than for anything he can give Luke, besides shelter and three square meals a day. Such is the fate of many children and adults who were once those children. But Luke is fortunate enough to have the wise elder, ObeWan Kanobie, intervene and take charge of his training as a Jedi knight.

One thing that makes *Star Wars* so engaging is that throughout the films Luke doesn't stop learning about himself, his past, and his absent father—and his psychological journey feeds a deep inner searching for many in the audience, not only for the lost father but for the lost self that withered in his and the cultural fathers' absence. In the wake of his initial victories against the Empire, Luke experiences an unexpected feeling of incompletion and dislocation. One would expect the victory against the Empire to lead him to be even more the externalized warrior. Yet even as the others celebrate the victory, he discovers the need to withdraw from the affairs of his people and even the duties of the soldier. He doesn't know it, but he is being called to the descent into himself, "the interior journey." Something seems to be wrong when he doesn't simply wear his success triumphantly. But his success on the battlefield has only made it possible for him to recognize the challenge of going inward and deepening his consciousness. The hero—the conscious individual—is able to hear the calling to further stages of initiation and maturity and not be distracted by the goings on or the needs of the group—at least at these vital junctures of his or her own development.

The way is not easy, nor are the road signs always marked. With a vague, intuitive hope of finding some sort of guidance through Yoda, the Zen-Leprichaunish Jedi master, Luke withdraws in search of what ends up being an isolated planet. At this critical moment, he does the right thing: he searches for a guide, someone who can—and who cares enough to—guide him into self-reliance and depths of himself he does not yet understand, someone to give definition and meaning to potentially chaotic and frightening developmental stages of life.

He was lucky to have found a mentor in Obe Wan when he first leaves home, and equally fortunate to find Yoda, who chastises Luke for always being in such a hurry to get elsewhere. Yoda knows that Luke cannot proceed in his maturation as a Jedi knight—or mature individual—until he faces his dark side, or shadow side. In psychological terms, he needs to integrate into consciousness his unconscious aspects, his repressed content, so that he can cross the bridge from childhood into adulthood, and be fully awake in the moment. This ability to be both mentally and physically present, is of course crucial to the survival of the warrior, the Jedi knight.

Even his name—Skywalker—cries out for an ordeal that will give him deeper grounding in himself. As Johnson describes it, "The shadow consists of those aspects of your character that belong to you but that have not been given any conscious place in your life" (*Transformation* 53). Luke has become a hero on the battlefield, in an extroverted realm. He now must make room for more inner spaciousness, for a deepening of the self that requires some degree of disengagement from the world and other people's opinions and expectations—the milieu through which he has up to this point known himself. It is a disengagement that enables us to return back home and know the place as if for the first time.

In a passage that does much to elucidate both Luke's journey and the journey taken by the dreamer through these dreams, Hollis discusses the underlying meaning of rituals stewarded by elder males and intended to initiate the son into self-sufficiency apart from mother dependence:

> Perhaps most significantly, the ordeal usually involved some form of isolation, a retreat to a sacred space away from the community. The essential part of being an adult means that not only can one not turn backward to the protection of others, but that one must learn to draw upon inner resources. No one knows he has them until he is obliged to use them....

> Ritual isolation is an introduction to a central truth, that no matter how tribal our social life, we are on the journey alone and must learn to draw strength and solace from within, or we will not achieve adulthood. Often the initiate spent months alone, waiting perhaps for the Great Dream, a communication from the gods as to his true name or proper vocation. He learned to depend on his wits, his courage and his weapons, or he perished.

> These rituals of passage were elaborate, wisely so, for they were extensive in direct relationship to the power of the mother complex, namely the enormous pull toward dependency in all of us...In traditional cultures the rites were more elaborate for boys than for girls, for girls were expected to leave their personal mothers but circle back to the hearth (19-20).

Yoda knows that much of the dark side that Luke must face consists of, as for every son, the shadow cast by the father; i.e. our experience of the father that we have not become conscious of. As therapist Robert Carlson observes, "We cannot get beyond where our fathers got on their journey to manhood until we confront our experience as sons."[2] What Luke doesn't know is that his father is Darth Vader, General of the Empire against which he risks his life in battle. The rebel's revolution against the Empire, which has pitted father against son, functions as a metaphor of the struggle to become a self separate from the parents.

Darth Vader
and the Dark Side of the Father

Vader is a prince of darkness figure who has gone over to the dark side of the Force, the Empire, the Corporation, and who is—it seems—almost entirely cut off from feelings of fatherliness, fraternity, and, especially, intimacy, and who, incidentally, also wears a uniform—like the fathers in three-piece suits of the previous dreams—that conceals his body, head and face. The faceless, black masked Vader thus becomes the perfect distant dark object on which every man and boy can project his deepest fears about the father. As such, Vader symbolizes the dark side of masculinity, the man who has given up intimacy for power, even if it pits him fatally against his own son. He ends up tragically alone.

The culmination of Luke's initiatory ordeal on the desolate planet in *The Empire Strikes Back* leads him underground into a cave, an image of initiation into our own unexplored depths. Here he unexpectedly confronts his greatest enemy. After a battle with light sabers, Luke cuts off Vader's head, and watches as his black helmet rolls away from his body and opens up to reveal his mysterious identity. But as he looks beneath the mask, it is Luke's own head and face he sees. He has met the enemy and it is all that he doesn't know about himself and his origins. In the cave we confront ourselves, especially what we have pushed away, called evil, rejected, and haven't wanted to look at. The shadow side we have not assimilated consciously (our experience of the father and mother) ends up operating in us unconsciously. Until Luke confronts the dark side of himself, he is susceptible to its seductive influences and a need to avoid it through exaggerated, compensatory actions—like Sir Lancelot's claims of spotless fidelity to a King Arthur he eventually betrays—and

---

2. Carlson, Robert. (1993, February). Editorial. *Seattle M. E. N.: Men's Evolvement Network*, 4

must betray if he is to develop as an individual deeper than a persona he wants to live up to.

We learn from Luke that until we face our shadow, and especially the part cast by the father, we won't be free enough to love him. Once Luke has "owned his shadow" by descending into the cave and confronting his father feelings, he becomes better grounded in himself, and doesn't need to act defensively toward is father.

One of the beautiful statements of *Star Wars* (which many sons hunger for) is that power and empire (corporation, social status) are not in the end as important as the natural bond between father and son.

In the last scene of the third film *Return of the Jedi*, as the Emperor is about to kill Luke, Vader intervenes, sacrificing his life to save his son, the consummate and, unfortunately, all too expected role of the father as protector. In the end, under his dark mask his denied need for closeness with his son finally wins out. It is very instructive and moving to go back and watch in the second and third films how by subtle degrees Luke's shift in consciousness, his awareness and appreciation of his own fears and needs, allows him to feel an almost unconditional love for his father—without abandoning his principles or his fight against the Empire. This is because once we own our feelings, we don't need to take others' actions personally, even our own parents'. It is also poignant to watch Luke's own transformation transform his father. With his dying words he asks Luke,

"Help me take off this mask, son, I want to look on you with my own eyes."

He has literally and figuratively opened up, become unmasked, and he and Luke share a moment of unguarded closeness. It will be their first and last, because, along the lines of many father-son scenes like this, the defenses and guardedness fall away only when the father or son is dying. As if in male culture one could only die for—not live with—this sort of closeness.

In the Disco

There is an important truth to recognize concerning the acting out of sexual impulses. At bottom an extramarital affair is a spiritual quest. A misdirected quest perhaps, but a quest nonetheless. A man who starts sleeping around is looking for spiritual renewal. He is looking in the wrong place, but probably because there are no ritual elders available in his life to guide him.

The same is true of any kind of acting out. The atmosphere in a bar or a honky-tonk is almost sacred—in that particular social situation there is a frank, perhaps forced attempt at communal cheer. Every person is treated as an equal, and all are searching for some sacred connection to the wellsprings of life.

—(Moore and Gillette, *Magician Within* 122)

The dream ego enters the cave of himself through—of all places—the dark, cavelike discotheque full of fraternity boys, stuck in what seems a robotic mode of unconsciousness. To this extent, the disco becomes a symbol of our lack of initiatory guides at this point in the fraternity boys' and the dreamer's psychological development, a place lacking initiation or meaningful opportunities for transit or transformation. So the disco in the dream instead becomes an informal tribal ritual of the extroverted search for soul, mixed with the powerful and sometimes compensatory searches for sex, companionship, ecstasy or some sort of physical release. The dreamer is looking for a way *inside* himself to a deeper level of consciousness or foundation of self, which the disco culture cannot satisfy. At a loss, he becomes resentful and desperate, feelings he externalizes as disgust toward the fraternity boys.

"Burning Rubber": Consciousness Spinning Its Wheels

The disco is filled with sexual imagery and excitation, yet the lack of awareness and communication makes for a lack of sensuality and connectedness to others, all of which puts the focus on externals: clothes, appearance, seduction: IMAGE. A culture-wide sensual deprivation has led to obsession with ideas and images of sex and success, (i.e. sensual deprivation leads to sexual obsession). For men especially, this has meant an obsession with the female body. In a world so rife with images and projections, there is psychological and spiritual stasis, lack of inner growth: consciousness spinning its wheels. This is what we do when we first get cars and can drive away from home, but don't really have any where to go. So we burn rubber, spin the wheels. Why is this? Burning rubber is a pretty aggressive thing to do. Maybe the sons are frustrated and angry that their fathers aren't initiating them into a more mysterious and adventurous experience of life, if they're initiating them into anything at all. In pre-industrial times, the fathers at least had the element of physical danger and survival on their sides, making initiation a much more immediately vital part of life for both father and son. Today, social roles and needs for initiation are less clearly defined

When the father is psychologically engaged in life and shares this with his son, anger and alienation are unnecessary. When this vital sharing doesn't happen, the sons drive off, burning rubber and "chasing pussy," angry at the fathers and dependent on the mothers, looking for some experience that will engage their depths. Ironically, men are now bonding over the fact that they never bonded with their fathers.

That the robotic young men are in a fraternity—literally a "brotherhood"—and at a disco seems to suggest that they aren't being adequately initiated from boyhood/brotherhood into manhood/individuality. Boys can't initiate boys; they need men, fathers, elders. Women, via the mother, initiate boys all day long into much of their psychic territory. But they don't have a man's body, a man's urges or the experience of being a man; the son needs to feed off his father's knowledge, not his absence. And it would be especially difficult for a mother to know how to initiate her son into separateness from *her*.

The beat in the dream emphasizes repetition. Without initiation into a deeper level of consciousness, this aspect of the dreamer is stuck in the repetition of adolescence, like the sons walking in circles in the first dream.

In what serves as a metaphor for the problems of machismo, these uninitiated young men mask their fear and uncertainty about themselves by "overpadding." They wear "glittery gold sports coats that exaggerate the size of their shoulders." Here the over padded sport coats and the three piece suit have come to symbolize—on a psychological level—dissociation from one's body and body of feelings, one's inner life and, usually, one's wound, as well as symbolizing a compensatory focus on image, externals. Thus we get trapped in maintaining an image of control, certitude and purposefulness.

Their attempt to look big and strong and in control only ends up "making their fist sized heads look even smaller," more grotesque. There is something grotesque in this attempt to mask insecurity and fear with machismo, and the dream presents this as a wrinkle or "distortion," Freud's term for a dream detail that calls attention to itself by its oddness. In the absence of older men to show them the way, these young men lack grounding and self-awareness, and try to compensate by emphasizing physical, sexual or other outward shows of strength that only become emblematic of what they lack.

The robotic movements impose an order or definition on what is actually a much more complex, ambiguous and confusing inner world that needs to be attended to much more mindfully if we are going to mature. But the flashy, cool guy image we adopt when we are uninitiated, i.e. self-alienated, goes against this sort of receptivity, humility and depth.

"Make-Up"

The female equivalent of machismo can involve "overpadding" as well: padding her bra to make her breasts appear bigger, "putting on her face," her mask, with mascara, lip-stick, eye-shadow, blush, foundation, dying her hair; wearing nylons, mini-skirts, high heels, flashy jewelry, breast implants, tummy tucks.... She has been pressured to live up to an image, sometimes sacrificing and *scarifying* her body as well, as currency for "success."

Needless to say, the gold glittery sport coats and exaggerated dance steps don't solve the fraternity boys' problem of the absent fathers. The dream ends up quipping about the fraternity boys' attempt to conceal their dis-ease with bravado by portraying their heads as fist-sized in proportion to the inflated jackets: the attempt merely makes them look ridiculous. These "fraternity" boys in every man hunger for initiation into an adulthood more meaningful and connective than a two car garage in suburbia and Super Bowl Sunday. Part of their dance is a dance of anger and fear. They need help moving from the aggressive extroversion of adolescence to a less egocentric consciousness capable of "engaging the world without defenses" (*Seat of the Soul* 23).

Without guidance into further stages of maturation, the fraternity brothers (and sorority sisters) in all of us keep us stuck revolving around a world of projection and fantasy, like the dancers beneath the revolving light ball. The disco is at once an image of the culture available to young men and women in college—a social scene which often doesn't do much to introduce them to inner resources—and it is an image of the dreamer's stasis and extroverted search for self.

So the disco in the dream becomes a metaphor for the extroverted self. The glittery light ball casts alluring but fractured gleams of light on the walls in a circular unchanging orbit and becomes perhaps the most apt metaphor for the disco mentality that revolves much but changes very little. There is a circularity about the pursuits that go on here, even amidst unmistakable energy and excitement. Often we go to the disco to desire or be desired by others, to pick someone up or get "picked up," revolving rather than evolving.

As his feelings of self-alienation increase, he starts to mock the fraternity boys and what he hears as a moronic beat. He is seeing in the fraternity boys a more exaggerated version of his own self-alienation. They dance "robotically" because they're still externalized, trying to live up to an image, not relating on an inner level to the music. Consequently, they have no rhythm and don't dance well.

The Shaman

> The [shaman] energy is the archetype of awareness, primarily, but also of anything that is not immediately apparent or commonsensical. It is the archetype that governs what is called in psychology "the observing ego."
>
> —(*King, Warrior, Lover, Magician* 106)

The observing ego is the part of us capable of being detached from our ego defenses, from our very personality, and is able to witness our various selves and reactions without acting. Its *action* is to observe and in that awareness create the space for transformation. This is the space into which the shaman rebirths the dream ego.

The shaman is by no means an unambiguous symbol. The older man's apparent unreliability re-enacts the dreamer's father-wound. Yet something changes. When the dreamer makes it perfectly clear by walking away that he won't tolerate any half-hearted attention, the older man is transformed into the shaman. It is as if the dreamer's refusal to accept anything less than the right quality of attention he needs creates the opportunity to get it

The fact that the shaman is a father figure who proves himself trustworthy in matters of the heart and soul cannot be overestimated, since the dreamer internalized unreliability as an attitude about men and himself.

The shaman uses gestures and eye contact rather than words, which are so often used to take the place of being truly present. He *embodies* his meaning, providing a masculine physicality which addresses the lack of masculine nurture in the dreamer's experience.

Unlike the sport coat clad fraternity boys, and the fathers of previous dreams, who all wear suit coats that conceal their bodies and their feelings, the shaman is almost naked. If clothes have become a metaphor in these dreams for how men are cut off from their bodies and feelings, the dream offers an antidote in the shaman who is psychologically present, unmasked, unclothed.

Like the moles, his symbolic predecessor in these dreams, he is comfortable underground, in the dark cave, and in his body. Symbolically speaking, he has integrated his shadow side into awareness, and so he doesn't have to spend time and energy avoiding it. That the shaman is black probably signifies the dreamer's shadow side. He is the only one who identifies with the dreamer's suffering. Perhaps his blackness signifies also the experience of the black man's suffering in America—his experience of abandonment, alienation and isolation on a social and familial level. The soul one must acquire to survive such suffering is akin to the shadow side shamen in all cultures must be willing to take on in order to be soul healers, spiritual visionaries. The shaman is a tribal figure, from a world where tribe means a community of individuals whose lives are perhaps more vitally interrelated on a psycho-spiritual level and dependent upon each other than in a modern industrialized capitalist society. Tribal societies, for all the primitivism and backwardness we perceive in them, at least integrate into their ways of survival a value of the individual's inner life and provide ritual initiation for the developmental stages of one's journey from birth to death. We have divorced economy from humanity, psyche.

Mythologically, the shaman is an underworld figure—like Poseidon or Hades—not easily distracted by the goings on of the surface. He occupies his own space, his own inner reality, and is thus able to help guide other people into theirs. He feels a correspondence between body and spirit and sees the soul as it is manifest in the individual's body, not just as an intellectualization. The shaman is able to focus completely on the dreamer's fear without himself becoming afraid or losing his sense of direction. The ability to bring awareness to things we normally fear and avoid is what makes a shaman a shaman. As Robert Johnson remarks, the shaman

> …understood that the human psyche is made up of energy flows and dynamic structures which can be brought into harmonious integration with one another. He called the structures he encountered demons, angels, or spirits. Today we would call the same things neuroses, complexes and archetypes. He conducted his research into the hidden worlds of nature and the psyche by altering his consciousness, often by drumming, and less often by the use of halluci-

nogenic drugs. His inward questing forced him to integrate his own fragmented psyche and confront his own complexes.

—(*Transformation* 70)

The shaman symbolizes the necessary introversion we all need. His ability to remain separate from the dream ego while still being with him and sharing his suffering implies a confidence that the son can make it on his own. Many mistake this form of distance in men as insensitivity and obliviousness, but in a mature man it expresses confidence in the younger man to get through the situation, and gives him enough space to make use of his own resources. But the older man has to be present and available or the son withdraws and rigidifies. Whereas the feminine or maternal response has traditionally been to immediately comfort and reduce another's suffering, this, perhaps, springing from a mother's sensitivity to her infant's helplessness, the masculine or mature father's response has traditionally come further away from the nursery, hunting, farming, building, fighting—where his measured detachment provides the son the opportunity to experience self-reliance.

Initiation:
The Death of the Ego
and the Guided Descent
into the Cave of the Self

The shaman is the most developed embodiment of the Magician [archetype] because of the problems he is willing to take on.

—Moore and Gillette (*Magician Within* 71)

A clawed hand takes the comfort-loving baby away,
and an adult warrior inhabits the body.

—Robert Bly (*Iron John* 151)

It is a difficult time in anyone's life, when the ways we have learned to live our lives in an ego controlled way fail to enable us to negotiate new and necessary depths of experience. To fail to bring awareness to this stage of life is to get stuck, to become stunted and stagnated, psychologically and often physically. The soul shrinks a little more when we don't answer the call initiating us into our depths. We move robotically to a repetitious beat, and begin padding our coats to cover up our insecurity or inflate an insecure sense of self. We loiter spiritually in the discos of sexual distraction or at dead ends when we're not ready for transformation or lack the guidance.

The ritual the shaman guides the dreamer through follows the basic pattern of male initiation or birthing rituals—something no longer formally ritualized in our culture. Typically, he is taken away from his mother by the elder males, and brought into the wilderness or a sacred space—often a cave—where he undergoes a simulated death, scarification, or an intense physical or psychological ordeal only to be reborn or brought back from the darkness through the men's care and understanding. Essentially, the ritual enacted in the dream amounts to a shamanic rebirthing wherein the young man is separated from his mother dependencies. This process makes it possible for him to become separate without having to become isolated. Symbolic rebirth through the male womb helps balance out the ferocious competitiveness he is often expected to show towards other men and guides him into a deeper sense of his own security apart from an intimate relationship with a woman. This symbolic grounding in himself is what makes healthy union with another possible and enmeshment less likely.

Without proper guidance from mature, caring elders—or a gifted therapist—suffering can feel meaningless, completely isolating, and defeat a person. The lack of this context from the fathers and from our culture in general has contributed to the tragic loss of many sons to physical and psychological isolation, drug abuse, alcoholism, crime and suicide—all of which men suffer at a rate four times that of women (Farrell).

The shaman ultimately symbolizes an attitude toward oneself. If we recall that the shaman has historically been the healer of lost souls, the visionary of a tribe, and the guide through the wounds, we can speculate that the shaman's presence in the dream is getting the dreamer in touch with this aspect of himself from which he has been cut off.

When the shaman says to the dreamer, "I know exactly what you're going through," the dreamer feels that his condition has finally been acknowledged and accepted. We are "accustomed" to feeling ashamed and isolated because of our wounds, which is why we have such an unconscious relationship to them. The shaman reverses this most destructive of all masculine paradigms. When the shaman looks the dreamer "piercingly in the eyes" it is the first time the dreamer has felt connected with anyone in the dream *through his pain,* and a stark contrast with his alienating experience in the disco and with his three-eyed girlfriend—to whom his inner reality is invisible.

Having his isolation understood and legitimized by the shaman leads the dreamer to a level of profound self-acceptance he hasn't experienced before. Thus having had his wound acknowledged, he is free to inhabit the spaciousness of self symbolized by the inner cave (and alluded to as the bean pod of the earlier dream) that we cover up when we become self-alienated in infancy and childhood.

In other words, when our inmost feelings have been shamed or neglected by our parents, our ego defenses grow over the entrance to the cave of the self, protecting yet isolating us from these rich inner spaces. This is when we create coping identities and defenses rather than cultivating an autonomous self and following our curiosities and passions, inhabiting the inner space that self-esteem brings. The descent wakes us up to the reality that the situation from childhood we had little or no control over has passed, and we can reclaim this inner space.

In the cave of the self, his ego—with all its defenses and projections layered up over a lifetime—has given way to a deeper level of self-acceptance, perhaps not experienced since birth. After a lifetime of pleasing others and defending ourselves from shame, this sort of self-acceptance opens us up to profound serenity and inner spaciousness. The expansive inner space of the cave of the self is the proper domain of the king who in the earlier dream is being kept in psychological storage in a bean pod.

The descent into the self or shamanic rebirthing involves what has been described as a "death of the ego," a process which when unstructured is too terrifying for us to endure. Robert Johnson, whose life work as a Jungian therapist has been to guide such psychological descents and transformations, describes this dark initiation into one's center as "requir[ing]

> that the ego consent to a subordinate, but still important role(70)....
> Jung described this moment of realignment as the relocation of the
> center of gravity of the self. This process is so painful, since it con-
> sists of dethroning the ego, that it is rarely done (71).... This reloca-
> tion appears to be death when viewed from the perspective of the
> ego (*Transformation* 84).

We can see the demands and restrictions of traditional masculinity as an "ego structure" which needs to be realigned by the individual, since it is a structure that both defends a man from pain but isolates him from inner space and from others.

Since the shaman (today's skilled therapist or counselor) has lived through the dark night of the soul and faced his dark side, he "has access to the whole terrain of the human unconscious." Because of this, Moore and Gillette identify the shaman archetype as the symbol of that part of us which is able to connect the conscious self or ego with our unconscious depths and potential:

> "…the shaman within every man…serve[s] as a conduit between the Ego and the unconscious" (*Magician Within* 109)

The Body of Feelings

The shaman takes the dreamer into his body where our deeper feelings—and deeper self—end up when we refuse to make room for them in consciousness. We in our minds may try to repress fears and feelings and rejected aspects, and even shape our bodies around these disowned aspects, but the feelings and experiences are still in the body. The body remembers. The journey into the body is especially important for men, who have for millennia subordinated their bodies and their feelings to the need to perform and compete in hostile environments.

There is a shape to fear. The body shapes itself to the anticipation of danger, becoming like a weapon to protect us from attack or rejection, pain, loneliness, depression—and even the thought of these. Unfortunately, shaped defensively, we close ourselves off from a wider range of both sensuous and psychological experience. We manifest our emotions—our consciousness—physically; our moods affect us on a cellular level. We store these fearful shapes in our bodies, which then take up the space in which we could really live, really resonate!—like a guitar so full of debris there's no space left for sound.

So when the shaman and the dreamer descend to the cave, there is a simultaneous entering into and acceptance of the body and the body of his hitherto rejected feelings—a body of information about who we are. This is expressed in the statement: "I feel places in my body I have never felt before." On the most fundamental level, where we resist feelings, we aren't in our bodies. And this is one of the most terrifying experiences of self-alienation imaginable. Of course, when we are most cut off from our bodies, we are least able to sense it.

We can trace this alienation from our sensual body to the father who is absent, or detached from his body, to cultural taboos that reinforce the use of our bodies as weapons and production and performance machines (and therefor shame or discourage sensuality,) and to the adolescent boy's need to separate from the mother and the external feminine—a move that becomes more tenuous and aggressive (more "all or none") the less guidance he gets from his father or older men. Another factor at play here is the pervasive idealization of the female body and the equation of femininity with nurture, nature, surrender, sensuality, and seduction—qualities, it seems, a man can express openly only if he defines himself as gay. Barring that, he represses these in himself and projects them onto women, his desire taking on the power of his inner alienation—the vacuum I mention in the opening. It would be interesting to explore how men's liberation from the disembodied performer paradigm changes their behavior in the bedroom; no longer needing to express his sensuality exclusively through her body, he too becomes the subject of touch and pleasure. *In Absent fathers, Lost Sons*, Guy Corneau describes this profound loss of our sensual body that results primarily from the lack of father affection from the earliest age:

> In the son's mind, men cannot allow themselves to touch, caress, smell, feel, laugh or cry, because these are things he has seen only his mother do. Later in his life, when he makes love, he will concentrate on genital pleasure and be careful not to let his excitement or playfulness go too far beyond the erogenous zones, for fear of acting too much like a woman. Only when he is completely alone will he allow himself a sensuality he considers shameful (24).

This is the sort of repression that led Freud to remark on the lamentable state of man, when, with an imagination and capacity for limitless sensuality, we end up experiencing less physical pleasure than the average dog. (*Civilization and Its Discontents*)

The Cave Image

It is no accident that the dreamer's initiation takes place inside a cave; archetypally, caves represent sacred spaces, womblike places of initiation and initiating transformation. Discussing ancient Grecian rites honoring Demeter, goddess of earth, Moore and Gillette remark:

> We find here again the use of an underground journey as a symbol for rebirth out of the earth's womb. Caves are used so often in initiation practices throughout the world it would seem the metaphor of cave as womb is an archetypal one. Initiation is a matter of dying to an outmoded Ego structure so that a wiser one can be formed...(*The Magician Within* 89).

The cave provides the protected psychological space necessary for undergoing the death of "an outmoded Ego structure" and for incubating the transformation into a new one. Being in the cave allows us to focus on inner realities that we are otherwise so easily distracted from or defended against when being in the outside world makes it unsafe to be open and vulnerable to inner processes. The cave is also where tribal societies found the sacred space to incubate their most important rituals. The cave of the psychologists office serves similar purposes today.

The Meaning of the Ritual

When the shaman and the dreamer come back outside the cave of the self, the shaman is wearing a ceremonial necklace made of sticks and bones, and his face is painted black and white with mud and ashes—materials of earth, death, grief and groundedness. The shamanic initiation is a penetration into psychological depths that we have been alienated from and thus unable to experience consciously. The re-birthing or soul retrieval ritual he performs shows the dreamer the axis by which he can reach and inhabit his inner space. This transforms his paradigm of self and security from an enmeshed pairing with m/other to a more grounded center within.

The presence of the spears suggests that now that the man has been initiated into his center—his masculine integrity, or inner kingdom alluded to in the Bean Pod dream—the need for making and enforcing adequate boundaries naturally follows.

The spear is a symbol of power and boundary-making. Spears symbolize the will of the warrior to define and defend his or her territory. This is true for us on a symbolic or psychological level; it doesn't mean we need to go out and buy guns or spears or become violent. In fact, the warrior's awareness of his or her needs and boundaries helps preclude violence, physical or emotional, because when we know our needs and limits, we are aware when our boundaries are violated before it's too late to have choices. When we know our needs and limits, we can consciously make the boundaries that regulate our connections to others, and save us from the all or none, distancing-enmeshment syndrome that characterizes so many unconscious relationships. Conscious boundaries also enable us to be intimate with another person, as it is only from distinctiveness that there can be union.

In the cave of the self we know what makes us happy, what we want and what we don't want in our lives, "how to spend the day." The spears suggest a need or ability to guard and protect this territory which was so hard to get to and so easily overrun by others when we were either too young or too unconscious to know better.

Often, the elaborateness of the ritual is less important on a literal level than it is to emphasize the need for transit from one level of consciousness to another. Though its meaning is ambiguous, the ritual of the spears is a symbolic aid intended to help remind the dreamer of his self-sufficiency. Two pairs of spears precede the fifth and singular spear, and each time after presenting these pairs to the dreamer, the shaman shakes his head—as if to suggest that the way back into himself is not through pairing with others, but through a more direct relationship to the self. Perhaps the two pairs of spears symbolize the two attempts the dreamer makes in the dream to bond or fuse with others as the means of establishing inner security: the unfortunate trip to bond with his father, and then taking these unresolved infantile conflicts to his girlfriend.

Only by making this inner connection as he has just done with the shaman's guidance and which is symbolized by the fifth spear, can he ever hope to be individuated enough from others to discover his own resources and at the same time be sufficiently separate and integrated to love another without holding her hostage to his lack. This happens simultaneously, not by isolating oneself. There is an important difference between separateness and isolation.

The Colors

That the spears are wrapped in red and white ribbon is of particular significance. Robert Bly and Michael Mead tell us that the colors red, white and black in myths and fairy tales correspond to stages of development in men and women. In fact, several weeks prior to dreaming this dream I heard Bly and

Meade at the Tacoma Men's Conference[3] talk about the significance of the colors. Red, which is usually the first stage for boys, signifies wildness, ferocity, aggression, outwardness, sexual passion. White being the second stage of development for boys and men brings in the less egocentric qualities of humility, selflessness, ideals, community. Black has to do with the less outward modes of the soul, the inwardness, contemplation and harder to reach depth that come with experiencing the deeper sometimes darker, events that "dethrone the ego" from the center of our being: death, loss, love, grief, limitation—that which deepen a person. The shaman himself is black, and brings the man into soul depths. Bly suggests that while the typical developmental sequence for males is from red to white to black, the typical sequence for women has been from white to red to black—a disparity that often causes men and women much confusion and grief (*Iron John* 199-206).

So while males typically begin in the red, full of outwardness and aggression, females traditionally start out in the more selfless white and heat up later, maybe in their thirties when they've stopped trying to please everyone and set about pleasing themselves. This sequence is definitely changing now, and more and more girls are starting out in the red.

That the shafts of the spears are wound in red and white ribbon suggests that the warrior qualities with which the dreamer protects his centeredness are not just passion, ferocity, and aggression. Rather, these sometimes necessarily aggressive strengths are tempered and integrated with the humility, ideals, selflessness and surrender of the white, less ego-oriented modes of being. But of course these are hardest for a man to cultivate when he has been taught to prove his self worth through assertiveness and stoicism. Red in the service of a selfish ego can do much violence, but when a person has integrated—intertwined, as the dream puts it—the white and the red his or her strength need not be self-serving, violent, or perhaps most important of all for men, isolated. The fatherless boys on Golding's island are stuck in the violent ferocity and egocentrism of the red without older men to introduce the white and make room for compassion and community.

The shaman is the symbolic—and in many tribes and cultures, the literal—guide into the cave, the soulful depths in ourselves which, after a life of dissociation and denial, must be entered through the wounds. This is particu-

3. Bly, Robert, and Michael Mead, Tacoma Men's Conference, Pacific Lutheran University, Tacoma, WA., June 18th, 1993.

larly true for men, who are culturally compelled to deny their woundedness and thereby become estranged from the experience the wound is covering.

6

The Cat's Wound
Healing the Man's Wounded Feminine Self

What is a scar? The native Americans have a magnificent tradition about scars, which Lame Deer alludes to briefly in his autobiography. I have heard the tradition said this way: "When you die, you meet the Old Hag, and she eats your scars. If you have no scars, she will eat your eyeballs, and you will be blind in the next world." That story moves awfully fast, but it certainly defends the value of scars.

If one has no scars, one becomes blind in the next world, but perhaps the man without scars is blind also in the imaginative world.

—Robert Bly (*Iron John* 215-16)

The Dream

I am with my father and brother, walking single file down a darkening road in an Industrial Park where my father managed a company when I was growing up. We walk without looking at or speaking to each other. My father is taking us somewhere, but hasn't told us where, so we follow silently until we come upon a building that is a combination of a little cottage and a huge warehouse. We climb the few porch steps to the door where we are greeted by an old woman my Dad seems to know well enough to exchange pleasantries. It might be his mother, but it's not clear.

As we start to go inside the old woman's house, her cat walks up to me and lets me rub her head. I notice the cat limping slightly, and a bald spot down her neck and chest where all the fur has been shaved off. As the old woman notices me notice this, she says in a high pitched nervous voice, "The poor dear just has a bad cold," to which my father nods his head animatedly in agreement while they turn nervously away, hoping I'll follow. But I see the cat is in great pain. She lies down on the porch on her side, exposing the ugly scar of an unhealed wound. Even though it is a violation of some unspoken rule, I move closer and, kneeling down under the porch light, see that the wound has been long neglected and is badly infected.

I feel squeamish and am about to back away when the cat reaches over to a dog which suddenly appears next to it, and grabs his paw and, with the dog's claw, tears open her wound. Fetid and rotten puss oozes out, and I almost get sick to my stomach. But as the puss gradually empties out, the wound starts to bleed a clear, pure liquid like gel. The cat instinctively begins rubbing the ointment on her wound with her paw, and as she does, she smiles and purrs deeply. The wound immediately starts to heal over.

*   *   *

The dream is about the opening of a wound long denied and covered up in the family. The wound can be many things. In this situation the silence and inexpressiveness between the father and sons leads to denial of a whole range of feelings, a denial which wounds, as the dream tells it, the dreamer's feline self, or feline energy—what we can for the moment expediently call his "feminine side." The dream also points to a denial of pain in general, and that perhaps this attitude was modeled for my father by his mother. The dream takes the dreamer back to familial origins. My father, brother and I walk through the industrial park where my father worked while I was growing up. In a sense, like so many other sons, we were trying to grow up while our father was away on business, and being away on business all the time probably wounded my father as well. This absence, inexpressiveness, and isolation between father and son leads to a wound which, in the dream, the father and his mother cooperate to pretend isn't there. They rush past the cat with pleasantries, but the observing ego refuses to play along any more. In a gesture of receptivity and self-acceptance, he kneels before the cat's wound, which is, of course, his own wound and perhaps a wound to men generations in the making.

When the dream ego stops to kneel before the wound, he is shown the seemingly paradoxical truth that only by opening up and relating to the wound does it begin to heal. The healing begins in awareness, not denial, defensiveness, or compensatory shows of bravado and strength which only close up the wound and make it fester. But when we've been socialized to base our self-worth and self-acceptance on external actions, it is all the more difficult to take the time to stop and kneel before our wounds, though they are the entrances to the deeper, rejected self. When we deny the wounds, the scars, as Bly refers to them above, we lose access to this inner spaciousness and commit ourselves more and more to self-alienation, rushing past the wounded cat pretending everything is fine.

Masculine and Feminine

As the overdevelopment of rational technology robs modern people of a sense of participating in nature, animal dreams seem meant to restore this sense of the natural to us, to compensate the peculiar state of soullessness that afflicts contemporary men in their search for that lifeless masculine ideal, the perfectly functional, rational life.

—Robert Hopcke (*Men's Dreams, Men's Healing* 24)

Once again the dreamer is visited by an animal, and once again we are reminded of the notion that when an animal comes to us in a dream, it's usually the right animal. That the dreamer is confronted with a wounded cat signifies that the "feminine" aspect of the man is wounded, or what our culture has considered "feminine." I use the terms "feminine" and "masculine" as expedients to refer to behavior we tend to be socialized into according to gender, not to refer to any sort of inherent capabilities that are biologically or gender determined. Without this distinction it is easy to mistake socialized behaviors for innate capacity, thereby reinforcing inaccurate stereotypical expectations of ourselves and each other which then become self-fulfilling prophecies. Nonetheless, the terms are useful in describing *socially constructed* or engendered realms of behavior.

Some of the most fundamental traditional gender expectations for the man as "success object" are that he be a competent performer or competitor both mentally and physically and thus externally or hierarchically oriented, rational, assertive, ambitious, industrious, and most of all detached from emotions that would get in the way of his ability to perform and compete, and fulfill the traditional social expectations that he provide, protect, and produce. All of which tend to cut him off from the behaviors traditionally expected of women (which tend to cut her off from the behaviors traditionally expected of men). Whereas he has been judged on the basis of his position in a social hierarchy, she is expected to be connective, relationship oriented, nurturing, empathic, receptive, passive, physically attractive, sensual, body and feeling awareness. For both men and women, these gender specific social expectations can come between the deeper relationship we each need to have with ourselves, cutting us off from vital expressions of the human psyche. I like Harville Hendrix's characterization of gender socialization in our country; he says, "men are still rewarded for being stoic and assertive and women for being cute and helpful" (*Keeping the Love You Find* 36).

We have come to a point in our evolution where it is no longer adaptive or healthy for men (or the new aggressive, "girls kick ass" woman for that matter) to be so externalized. In a profoundly revealing passage of his book, *Men's Dreams, Men's Healing*, the Jungian analyst and writer Robert Hopcke discusses the myth of Hades' abduction or rape of Persephone as an illustration of the dire consequences to the man's psyche when acceptable human behaviors are divided into masculine and feminine, and more specifically, when the behaviors associated with Eros (love) or relationship are defined as inherently feminine and prohibited in men. In that myth, carefree Persephone, daughter of Demeter (goddess of earth) is walking through the fields when the god of the underworld, Hades, opens up the earth and steals her for his wife, presumably to bring love and femininity into his dark and loveless, more "masculine" world (an attempt perhaps to furnish the underground men's room):

> By categorizing Eros—feeling, relationship, sensitivity, and passion—as "feminine" and thereby assigning such qualities literally to women or figuratively to the feminine, in some archetypal sense men find themselves alienated from the true fullness of psychic life and instead identified with a conception of masculinity in which force, control, and performance are substituted. *The stage is set for rape [both literal and symbolic—my insert and italics] as a brutal and ultimately unworkable "solution" to this painful split in men, in which men seek to penetrate and obtain for themselves literally or emotionally those qualities that have been given away to women* (95).

Furthermore, we have seen how women are coerced into performing for men those social and emotional functions that the anima as archetype performs in the psyche; they serve as the carrier of relationship and the embodiment of soul as passion, sexuality and life. The release of women's bondage to femininity provides freedom and cure for men as well as for women. To go even further, we have seen how these sex role assignments rest upon an even more basic condition within a patriarchal society, namely, men's alienation from their own inner wholeness as men (100).

Through his socialization as a man, he becomes alienated from the qualities in himself that are, in our culture, idealized and sanctioned as feminine: sensitivity, nurture, sexiness, sensuality, compassion, tenderness. Cut off from these in himself, he becomes convinced he can't survive without the external feminine—mother, lover, wife, madonna, whore—and is thus led by this faulty belief (reinforced by the absence of a nurturing father or older male(s) and idealized images of women casting her as everything he is cut off from in himself) to possess her, feel threatened by her separateness and full expression. I call this condition emotional or psychological hostage taking—a move analogous to Hades' mythic abduction of Persephone, which is at heart a tragic compensation for having been alienated from aspects of ourselves. Of course, women do this with men as well, expecting the man to be less needy and emotional, more stoic, to sacrifice his needs in order to provide (for her), protect (her) produce and perform (for her), that is to provide for her what she unconsciously agreed to cut off from in herself to be "feminine." But because she has been expected to be relationship oriented, her self-alienation usually doesn't isolate her as brutally as it can isolate men, from others, yes, but more importantly from his own ability for self-nurture and self-love, what Hopcke refers to as "men's alienation from their own inner wholeness as men." Perhaps this is why men fare so much worse than women outside of relationships, developing, as I've noted earlier, drug and alcohol addictions, disease, and committing suicide at alarmingly higher rates than women.

Hopcke observes that "patriarchal conditioning robs men of an ability to relate to their own soul, locating their wholeness in women, in relationship to women (101)." This precarious situation occurs in the previous dream when the dreamer attempts to get, through the three-eyed woman, the nurturing relationship he needs to have with himself. This is possibly the most fundamental problem in male socialization. It is tempting for each gender to resent the "privileges" they perceive to be the easy birthright of the other. Societal expectations are at odds at some point with the needs of the individual, and this is reflected in both genders. The list above, however partial and sketchy, indicates profound differences between masculine and feminine culture—though it says nothing about the psychological or behavioral capacities of either men or women. Once again, I describe a culture, not a gender. What our culture and family have separated into gendered realms, the individual must work to integrate into balance within him or herself. However far reaching might be the psycho-biological differences or predispositions between men and women, we share a far deeper commonality as beings who need to love and feel loved, and be meaningfully engaged in life. The deeper we go as individuals the less we are defined by our gender, and especially social conditioning based on gender. Guy Corneau adds to this point:

> Vulnerability, feeling, intellect, strength and courage do not belong exclusively to either men or women. These qualities are the common heritage of humanity. As Maurice Champagne-Gilbert states, "...[men's] real challenge lies in...a new relationship in which the values traditionally labeled as feminine are repossessed by men as existential values" (*Absent Fathers, Lost Sons* 175).

Feminists have for decades been reclaiming values traditionally considered masculine, which has made both possible and *necessary* a similar movement for men.

According to the dream, the man must bring himself into a more receptive and conscious relationship with his feminine qualities, even if this involves acknowledging that he is wounded and being willing to go into the wound, tear it open—the unseating of the ego and the penetration of ego defenses.

Many men and women go through life alone, turning themselves into enclosures, defensive ego structures (to protect themselves against unconsciously anticipated trauma), for which the cat's infected festering wound becomes the perfect metaphor. The violence of the confrontation with our woundedness increases to the degree to which we have been repressing it. Not relating consciously to the wound keeps it closed, and keeps us isolated from a more intimate relationship with ourselves and others. As in the earlier dream where the mole bites the dreamer into a more conscious relationship to himself, a wounding must take place in the psyche to get through the ego's defenses and reach these repressed aspects. The cat knows what to do: a new wounding opens up the old festering wound so it can begin to heal; this is a commentary on denial and avoidance in general. What has been rejected and denied in us must be brought into the light of awareness—according to the dream, brought under the porch light and related to consciously. The ego needs to be relativized, partially surrendered, in order to expand.

> *The cat lies down on the porch on her side, exposing the ugly scar of an unhealed wound. I move closer to the cat and, kneeling down under the porch light, see that the wound has been long neglected and is badly infected and festering.*

> *I feel squeamish and am about to back away when the cat reaches over to a dog which suddenly appears next to it, and grabs his paw and with the dog's claws tears open her wound.*

The dream also suggests—in a curious union of what we commonly consider mortal enemies—that the cat needs the dog to help open its wound; we can't heal alone. Cat needs dog, self needs others, masculine needs feminine in order to achieve wholeness. Just as the cat needs the dog to open its wound, the man needs to be relating to his wounded or repressed self, and he also needs to be relating to his wound through others. Alone it is too easy to seal ourselves off from our wounds to avoid them, thereby covering up our deepest sensitivities and capacities. In relationship to others, our wounds get torn open, and we are forced to relate to more of ourselves. This is when we need most to relate to them and what they represent in ourselves receptively, as if kneeling before them with compassion and acceptance.

We might see the cat and the dog as symbolizing masculine and feminine characteristics: the "feminine" aspects of the individual need to be brought into relationship with the "masculine" aspects—with the ego; and the observing ego, the part of us able to kneel receptively before our wounds, is the right part of the self to oversee this reconciliation. The observing ego is associated with the shaman archetype of the last dream. The denouement of the dream occurs when the dreamer kneels down before the wounded cat, the image of his own wound, in a gesture of acceptance, humility, and descent. It has taken him most of his life to reach this point, and he has had to overcome cultural and familial denial to get here.

My father, brother and I walk through the darkened industrial park not looking at or speaking to each other; *the condition of being cut off from each other is associated with the industrial park, and the work men are expected to do.*

Robert Hopcke, who has worked extensively with men in therapy, describes the most general wound of masculinity, or what he specifies as "patriarchal" masculinity, as a wound to their feeling awareness. Most of his male clients

> ...begin their work...treating their difficulties as mechanical prob-
> lems to be repaired, a process into which the inner life of their feel-
> ings enters not at all. And no feelings about having no feelings. The
> anesthesia of male socialization, I have found, is still quite effective.
> For this reason, unless given evidence to the contrary, I find myself
> often devoting the better part of the first year of therapy with a male
> patient simply to the development of a workable emotional aware-
> ness. Interns I supervise, especially female interns, find themselves
> incredulous when I tell them that it might take that long for a man
> to acquire what I would consider the basic tools of therapy: emo-
> tional awareness, a sufficiently discriminating feeling vocabulary to
> express what they are feeling, and sometimes hardest of all to
> develop, the necessary trust with me to actually feel the feelings in
> the therapy room (*Men's Dreams, Men's Healing* 12).

Given the current trend of the masculinization of women, the analysis herein is increasingly applicable to women.

Killing the Cat Within:
The Cat Came Back

The act of kneeling down before the wounded cat reverses a lifetime of defensiveness and self-denial, and symbolizes the possibility of integrating into oneself what has been banished, censored and shamed.

But I was not always so receptive to wounded cats. Over a period of ten years preceding this dream I was visited by a cat in a series of dreams in which I am required by some agonizing yet inexplicable imperative to kill it, over and over, dream after dream. To make matters worse, the cat resembles closely my family's first cat—Hairy—to whom I was very attached as a child and infant and to whom we showed more affection than to each other. So cats came to represent for me a deep animal-childlike sensuality, affection and connected-ness to others. In these dreams, the cat is always wounded in such a way that it can neither live nor die. The cat always comes suffering unspeakable agony which disturbs me greatly but which I am not able to understand. It throws me into in an agonized state of internal struggle, unsure if the imperative to kill the cat and put it out of its misery is the right thing to do, even though in dream after desperate dream it is what I am *expected* to do.

In the first such dream, typical of the rest, I am racing in a bicycle race against a field of other men, trying to beat a DEADLINE, when a cat crosses my path and I am forced to stop and get off the bike. I must kill the cat with a fork and eat it or I won't be able to rejoin the race. Even the thought of this is terrible, but in the dream it is understood that there is no other choice. The cat's suffering is too great for me to do anything with except kill, because I have to get back to the race or I'll be a failure, which is not conscious in the dream, but experienced as a compulsion. The feline side of my psyche, in the form of a cat, attempts to interrupt my dogged race to beat the deadline; the repressed feminine side has come to disrupt the destructive, competitive trap I am in. But I have become so cut off from this wounded, sensual feline side of myself, the only way I have known how to relate to it is by pushing it out of consciousness, repressing it, trying to kill it—an act toward the psyche which guarantees it will return with renewed force.

The need to kill the cat so I can rejoin "the race" represents the masculine imperative to perform at all costs—to let no emotions or needs get in the way of the performance by which he is unconsciously convinced he must prove himself worthy of love—someone else's love. This is a catch twenty two that keeps his search for love and his experience of sensuality externalized. Ironically, by pushing all these natural feelings, impulses and sensuousness out of his mind they become the very things that end up getting in the way of his ability to "perform" well.

So here the principle of hierarchy associated with patriarchal masculinity represses the principle of connectedness, often associated with traditional feminine culture. The dream reveals the extent to which his masculine side—which characterizes his ego—is in opposition to his more unconscious and wounded "feminine" side.

The man opposes his own more "feminine" qualities because his socialization has shamed them into hiding; but there is another source for this opposition, and it manifests itself to the extent a man is unsure of his own autonomy as an individual, or his *integrity* as a man. When the son doesn't bond properly with his father, the consequent enmeshment with his mother makes it extremely difficult for him to express and *integrate* feminine qualities. Unable to model his masculinity on his father, he is left unsure of his own. And unsure of his own masculinity, he experiences the feminine alternately as something he fervently desires, needs and as a dependence or engulfment which threatens his dubious autonomy. He fears being devoured by his mother and the feminine and any of the characteristic behaviors he associates with the world of females. In love, this fear gives birth to the dance of distancing and enmeshment. Add to this engulfment fear the collective shaming by his peers and elders of anything sissy pussy, femmy, or homo—and the death blow to his feline/feminine side is struck early and often. Hence the vacuum is created in the psyche which fuels the externalization of his femininty in women and the unhealthy dependence that ensues.

The world he is about to enter as an adolescent and young man tells him that he can't remain tied to his mother through his childhood dependencies; yet the father or fathers aren't present enough to help guide him into a more self-assured separateness that is still connected to women. Being unsure of his own masculinity and autonomy forces him into a polarized opposition toward, yet dependence on, all things female. (Hence the inexplicable need in the dreams to kill the cats he loves.) When he accepts the feminine in himself and integrates it into consciousness, he will stop playing out this tortured self-division on himself *and* the women in his life. Until then, his repression effectively cuts him off from his own inner capacities for expressing a whole range of behaviors: nurture, affection, needs, fears, spontaneity, playfulness, sensuality.

When we don't express our own "feminine" qualities, we remain isolated in our ego quests (bike races, deadlines, shut up in windowless factories) to win like a hero the love of the princess while simultaneously killing the qualities in ourselves we so fervently desire that she give us.

In the dream, the cat crosses my path so that I have no choice but to get off my bike, leave the race and reckon with this wounded part of my psyche. In an agonized moment of what I am convinced is necessary for my survival, I kill the cat with a fork and symbolically eat it. In a sense, I do need to eat the cat to take it inside myself, digest or internalize the qualities it represents, so I don't keep locating the "feminine" outside myself where it reinforces dependence and lack of inner wholeness. Of course, killing the cat in my dream won't put it out of its misery; my attempts to kill it, dream after dream, only prolong and intensify its and my own suffering. The cat and all it represents in a man's psyche wants to be related to, integrated into consciousness. But at twenty-something, I had, like Robert Hopcke's men, experienced no initiation into my "emotional awareness," and thus had no room for deeper needs not associated with performance. When we don't relate to this whole range of feelings in ourselves, they become part of the threatening Other, and must be opposed, possessed or controlled in others.

"Sex Kittens"

It is a sad measure of my socialization that I am convinced my very survival and success depend on killing this part of myself, and that I feel the only option I have is to 'put it out of its misery'. I don't consciously understand in the dream that this unbearable drama I keep reenacting is a personification of the way I relate to myself, and the psyche's way of forcing into consciousness the content I have been trying to control and repress most of my life. My struggle is not with the cat, but with the part of myself that is more prepared to *kill* it than *be* it. A man's socialization often teaches him to control his more natural cat-like body-mind processes and presence to fit into the business suit, the industrial park, subordinate all of his wondrous curiosities and desires—so abundant in childhood—to beating the deadline and winning the race. So alienated from and hostile to this in ourselves, we require or desire women to be cat like, sensual, seductive—"sex kittens."

The Unbearable Imperative to Always Perform

The wounded cat comes to get the dreamer's attention focused on the loss of self that maintaining such a closed competitive ego is costing him. He doesn't have time to do what it is asking him to do, which is be present, in his body and in his feelings, because doing this would mean withdrawing from the race he was taught he had to win to be a man. This convergence of conflicting gestalts puts many men in a painful double bind, and most won't withdraw from the race unless they are interrupted by more vicious manifestations of this exiled self—heart attacks, colon cancer, divorce, depression, death.

Once again, Robert Hopcke's experience with men in therapy warrants reference here. He recalls a client's dream which has remarkable parallels to the cat and other animal dreams herein. The client dreams about lying in bed motionless while a line of ants crawls through his house onto the bed and all over his body. Hopcke sees in the man's reaction to these little hard to control creatures men's "patriarchal" programming to "exterminate" all feelings that are not related to control and performance. The fact that this excerpt describing another man's dream fits mine as well is testimony to a shared expectation that we show a stoic hostility to our inner life when it gets in the way of performing the roles of provider, producer, protector:

> To let one in is to let in a horde, and so all feelings must be exterminated if the status quo is to be maintained, if life is not to be disrupted. Of course, the irony of this extermination ethic is that, by refusing to participate in the realm of the animal where soul and instinct meet in nature, men find themselves wrapped ever tighter in hermetically sealed cocoon of control and isolation that disrupts their lives more completely than the more natural disruption posed by the presence of fellow creatures on earth (25).

I remember when I used to be the exterminator of my own feelings. I was in a dry sort of agony that I couldn't even express through tears. It ends up taking more energy to oppose and control our more natural processes—physical and psychological—than it does to be aware of them, even when these processes seem to threaten our plans and the image of self and order we become attached to. Guy Corneau's remarks about the usefulness of depression to jar us out of our solipsistic notions of ourselves applies well to dreams, and especially to the visitations of dream animals. "We should acknowledge their role in saving us from an unreal world in which everything is in our own image" (*Absent Fathers, Lost Sons* 165). The cat comes to estrange me from my more ego-bound strategies of relating to myself and the world, strategies which are reinforcing my psychological isolation. At the time of the dream I was still too invested in the obsessive-compulsive performer role to be receptive to the cat, though it is remarkable to me that the dream seems to have known the cure twenty years before I understood the problem.

The Cry for Help:
Breaking the Silence and Isolation

Nearly ten years after the "Deadline" dream and a year preceding "The Cat's Wound" dream, I dreamed the last in a long line of the cat killing dreams. In the dream, I find myself sitting at the family dinner table with two of my sisters. My father arrives. We discuss what we're going to have for dinner, and he decides we'll go out to eat. He and my sisters leave, and I am left alone at the table. A black cat is laid out on her side in the center of the table, its eyes tilted upward. She looks dead, but is barely alive. Once again I am supposed to kill the cat, and this causes me unbearable agony. That this happens at the dinner table suggests it might be part of the family diet, psychologically speaking.

There is a sense in the dream that it is my unquestionable duty to kill it; that is why I'm left alone with the wounded cat. Caught in the same double bind I experience in the earlier cat dreams, I can't contain the agony any longer. I run out of the room and cry out to my sisters for help. But instead of feeling like an irredeemable failure, as I fear, I feel an unexpected relief. A great burden is lifted. I have failed to live up to this code of stoic denial—and become more human. This immediately breaks the unbearable isolation and connects me to others.

The fact that in the dream I experience this pressure to kill the cat as an inexplicable imperative I have no choice whatsoever except to obey indicates that as a man, and as my father's son, I had internalized it unconsciously, swallowed it whole. The dream brings me face to face with a masculine and familial injunction so pervasive and yet so unconscious I can't see it objectively; the primary function of the dream is to make the dreamer conscious of this unconscious part which is ruling his life.

In the dream, I am unable to defeat, prevail over, contain or control the "problem" that the cat represents. It is bigger than me, deeper than my soldierly stoicism, my Herculean willpower, all the ego strategies I was taught I needed to survive and succeed and which wear so many masks in our culture and lead so many men and women into isolation and rigidity. The dream presents to me, as did many dreams before, this more sensuous side of myself that would connect me intimately with life but that seems to threaten the performance by which I unconsciously assume my worth will be judged. Hence, the seeming impossibility of the struggle. The attitude most needed in these situations is what I as a boy and a man was shamed most from ever doing: surrendering, i.e. not *doing* anything. As I have mentioned earlier, this is a case when, in Jungian terms, "Our Ego structures are particularly inadequate to face our changing circumstances" (*Transformation* 117), and the ego must be unseated, knocked off its bicycle, so to speak. But unless we find or are guided into an alternative way of proceeding, most of us go on in "quiet desperation" trying even harder to make the old unconscious ways work. Coming into new consciousness of ourselves is not easy; we need support, and this is not easily come by if we're still trying to beat the deadline or win the race, or if the people around us shame us when we do get off the bike.

Crying out breaks us out of the isolated ego quests that doom us to lonely lives and dependence on others for love and sensuality. At the brink of sanity and in violation of the rules I internalized as a man to "get the job done" and "go it alone," I cry out for help from my sisters—the personification of the more connective, empathic side of myself organized around the Eros principle. The dream reveals how important expressing our fear is to breaking the destructive pattern of inexpressiveness and isolation.

The dream is reminiscent of a scene in one of western culture's central myths—the Grail legend from the Tales of King Arthur. At the end of the long quest for the Grail chalice which would supposedly restore life to the kingdom, Percival, the last remaining Grail knight, meets the Fisher King who invites him to dinner at the Grail castle. The Fisher King is wounded (like the cat) such that he cannot die yet cannot live fully—a wound to his "thigh" or genitals, to his masculinity or manhood. The king's wound can be healed only if a guest speaks out at the dinner table about the strange sight he witnesses there of blood dripping off a lance into the grail chalice. Percival sees the vision but "has promised his mother he would hold his tongue in society" (Corneau 159), so he resists the urge to speak openly to the king. The spell remains unbroken and the king goes on suffering in silence and isolation. In the Cat's Wound dream, the mother has also taught her son (my father) not to speak of the wound.

Percival's silence maintains his and the king's mutual isolation and prolongs the king's suffering; the wound remains closed off, unshared, unhealed. We walk silently through the darkened streets of the industrial park not looking at or speaking to each other, sharing the same fate of silence and inexpressiveness.

Breathing Under Water

Late, by myself, in the boat of myself,
no light and no land anywhere,
cloudcover thick. I try to stay
just above the surface, yet I'm already under
and living within the ocean.

—Rumi, Quatrain #12

When I left college in my early twenties, I began having a series of dreams about almost drowning under water. At that time I was very driven to prove myself by doing something important or extraordinary, yet deeply unsure what I wanted to do or be in life. The need to become something great or attain important status in the world (i.e. get my father's attention and approval) had eclipsed any direct awareness or exploration of what made me happy. So tense and anxious had I become at this time that I began to have episodes where breathing was difficult; at times I would literally be gasping for breath, yet there was no medical reason for my labored, shallow breathing. There were times, lying on my bed staring at the ceiling or pacing my room that I thought I was going to suffocate.

During this time I had a series of dreams in which I am under water in a myriad of scenes running out of air and unable to breathe. I wake up in "real" life having stopped breathing—a terrifying experience that each time made me afraid to go back to sleep. Near the end of this dream series, my sister Cynthia, who is a year younger than I and with whom I was close growing up, begins appearing. In each of the dreams, she swims or walks up to me underwater, able to breathe with ease. Her presence in the dreams takes away the terror, but not the fact that I end up out of air and unable to breathe. In the last under water dream she appears to me just as I am running out of air. But this time my curiosity is larger than my fear. As she swims up to me, I watch her to learn the secret of breathing under water. She looks at me compassionately yet confidently and says, "It's OK. Just breathe." Thus assured, I relax and, to my astonishment and great relief, realize I am already breathing under water. I walk around on the sea floor taking in the sights, at ease and full of wonder.

We could say that my anima or "feminine" side—personified in the dream by my sister—comes to me to guide me into a depth of being that I was not familiar with at that time of my life, and was thus drowning in, namely, being able to just BE without my self-acceptance having to be based on performance, being a "success object." Without the observance of self that comes out of self-acceptance, we never have the opportunity even to listen to what makes us happy. I was trying too hard to succeed at things that had no connection to the deeper needs I had been ignoring. According to the dream's symbolism, when our lives are so driven by external proofs, we aren't able to inhabit ourselves comfortably; that is, we are unable to breathe under water. Where there is lack of self-acceptance on the inner level, the rhythm of our whole being is thrown out of whack, becomes shallow and labored. And it is no surprise that this would manifest itself in one's breathing. Breathing is almost synonymous with our existence. In many languages the word for "breath" is the same word for "spirit." How we breathe manifests how we hold ourselves or inhabit our bodies, our lives. Many types of meditation have for thousands of years been based on this truth.

When Cynthia tells me, "It's OK. Just breathe," she may just as well have said to me, "It's OK. Just *be*," since the dream addresses an existential crisis or self-alienation (and alienation from the body) brought on by the increasingly anxious search for identity or self in a totally externalized way. The dream is about letting go of the need to be something to get the approval of others, and about settling into the deeper self (the water, the unconscious) where we can just Be, just breathe. Water is so often associated in dreams with our unconscious, transformative depths as to be the main archetype of one's unconscious.

Breathing under water becomes symbolic of being able to be in the psychological depths we once feared would drown us if we let go, inhaled. For a man conditioned to be goal-driven and defined by social status rather than connectedness, breathing under water might mean letting go of control and plans and purposefulness enough to let himself just be aware of his body and mind, his emotions, what makes him happy, excited, afraid, curious. Being able to breathe under water represents being able to be at this deeper, more mindful level in oneself where observation is a worthy action. After this dream I no longer suffered shortness of breath. It is also the time I began to explore free time and the strange anxiety many of us have when faced with freedom, and it was in the depths of these moments that I finally began painting, sculpting and playing music.

The Industrial Park

The dream takes place in the same Industrial Park where my father worked in "real" or waking life, and where, several generations ago, the father-son bond began to break down as the industrial revolution took fathers away from family land, farms, cottage industries (the cottage in the dream) and shops and into factories—replacing a more neighborhood or home-based autonomous life with a time clock and a corporate order.

So the Industrial Park (quite a telling euphemism in itself, since there's not much time for recreation in this "park") is associated with the wound of being abandoned by the father. It is also the place where the father often becomes alienated from himself, his time, his body, his wife, children, and, perhaps most importantly, the child within himself (or inner king).

Such an economy and social organization, really, represented by the industrial park, values performance, profit and efficiency over soul and community, over making time for the inner life and connectedness to others. This, in fact, was Marx's most serious criticism of capitalist societies, that they turn workers into commodities, and value people primarily in terms of production, not as sentient individuals. The worker, whether in a socialist or capitalist country, learns to value—or rather devalue—himself in these terms. In a word, he becomes alienated from his deeper self, at least at work, and this estranges him and alienates him from this deeper humanity in others.

We are so accustomed to the profit motive as the organizational principle of our society that we accept events like the traumatic displacement of people and their families when workers are laid off to preserve profits as if they were inevitable, and not the consequence of priorities, values and decisions by people. The need to survive in an economy that doesn't value the soul wounds all of us, and that is for each of us to recognize and heal in our own way. Jungian psychology suggests that the healing of the self via awareness of one's complexes at least helps keep one from dangerously projecting one's inner conflict onto others. When we are not aware of our complexes, our "repression" becomes our "oppression" of others, our self-estrangement becomes resentment of others, our unconscious self-hatred becomes hatred of others.

In the Industrial Park, the father becomes alienated from a big part of himself, and passes this estrangement on to his sons, who walk in single file in silence and darkness.

Kneeling

What many men find, especially in these changing times, is that the insight and efficacy of the Logos principle [knowledge, control, power—my insert] can only take them so far, and thus, often, must cede its place to Eros, to the healing born of relationship and all that relationship entails: responsibility, vulnerability, interdependence, feeling, love, creativity, work, acceptance of imperfection, and abiding care and nurture.

—Robert Hopcke (*Men's Dreams* 83)

Despite the family pressure in "The Cat's Wound" dream to leave the wound alone, the dreamer follows the cat out onto the porch and gets down on his knees to get a closer look. In the dream this takes a second. In "real" life it could take years, decades, sometimes generations for a man to kneel alongside his wounds. He is likely up against a pattern of denial and self-alienation generations in the making. This sort of mindfulness is the only way of ending the cycle of denial and repetition.

"The Cat's Wound" dream embodies the paradox of pain: that out of the heart of the wound comes the ointment we need, psychologically speaking. Feeling it is healing it. No wound can be healed by covering it up. Kneeling before the wounded cat involves no less than a transformation of consciousness, a relocation of the center of the self from the defensive controlling ego to the receptive observer capable of kneeling before his wounds. This locates the feminine in the proper place—within himself!

Going into our wounds relieves us of the need for detours, denial and circuitous defensive systems. Bly says that when we start to grieve over our own wounds, we give up blaming others. This is because the wound reconciles us with whatever we've disowned in ourselves. Closing off the wounds only preserves them and commits us to performing or always being "cheerful" to compensate for the vacuum within. When we can openly express our grief we are relieved of the rigidity and isolation of a defensive, closed ego. This is what Bly means when he says, in *Iron John* that men must learn to "limp in public". This breaks the tradition of stoicism, and frees us to express the strength that comes from connectedness and relationship—rather than exclusively hierarchy and control.

The cat dreams then symbolize his making room for the qualities in himself we associate with the feminine but that are the birthright of humanity, of each individual regardless of gender.

The Cat Image

In considering what the dream presents as the unconscious state of things to the dreamer and his therapist, it is often fruitful to consider how close to human a dream animal is in order to get a sense of how hard a patient might need to work to relate to whatever instinctual processes the dream animal symbolizes for him psychologically.

—Robert Hopcke (*Men's Dreams* 24)

We have discussed the symbolism of the cat as the dreamer's wounded feminine side. The cat perhaps manifests other qualities or "instinctual processes" that might help the masculine become more whole. First of all, the cat is not afraid to relate to her wound. She knows that only by opening it will the wound begin to heal. And she doesn't hesitate to reach out for help, even from a dog, whereas a man's "pride," as we euphemistically call the self-abusive pressure his culture puts on him and he ultimately puts on himself to do it alone, might prevent him from admitting he's hurt, let alone asking for help.

The next part of the process of healing is really about preventative medicine. And the cat is the right animal to teach us this as well. The cat represents an animal very at home in its body, living in its body much more than humans live in their bodies, in the sense of living its consciousness through its body and not just through intellect, reason and the abstract map we make our world into. While she becomes immersed in her body and physical habitat, we are so often in our heads, our words, bound up and constructed by a language of manipulating, defining and planning the future that disconnects us from our senses, the immediate environment and moment. Abstract conceptualization is a remarkable ability when balanced with other modes of awareness, but an impoverishment of life when it comes at the exclusion of our intuitive, animal body awareness.

Whereas we can often outrun our own physical limits by imposing unhealthy conditions on ourselves for success, a cat will only push its body to its limits if it's a matter of life or death. Otherwise, its normal concern is getting the maximal pleasure from, or I should say, through it. Sleeping, sunning, sniffing, stretching, purring, growling, grooming its coat, climbing trees, hunting birds, rubbing up against bushes and people—the cat indulges its full range of senses, drawing us closer into a more animal intuitive relationship with it, ourselves and the world.

Humans, meanwhile, spend very little time with their consciousness centered in their bodies, much less deriving much information through their body's relationship to the natural world. The cat symbolizes a consciousness or way of being that is much less mediated and blunted by technologies such as cities, cars, computer screens, alarm clocks and television that come between us and a more direct relationship with the physical, three-dimensional world.

We have moved so much of our consciousness from our bodies into abstract thinking and manipulating outcomes in the external world,[1] and we no doubt have had to do much of this in order to survive and maintain the world we have created. Now it seems in order to save our and other animals' habitats from destruction, we must balance this cunning, abstract manipulator out with the more receptive, intuitive animal that exists in its body in the moment in harmony with its habitat. Destroy the habitat, as we are doing, and we lose the measure and reminder of all that is not us, all that would enlarge our sense of existential possibilities, all that would, ultimately, remind us of

---

1. We think our mind, our consciousness, is in our brain—logical, rational, deductive, word-based—because we have grown so dependent on these functions to run the machine we have made our world into. But our brain is part of our mind, our mind part of our body, our body part of a connectivity to our habitat. Fingers, hands, eyes, ears, nose, skin, legs, feet, shoulders, thighs, elbows, arms, lungs, intestines, bowels, heart are all extensions of our mind, all inescapably part of the way we come in touch with the world and ourselves, and thus inescapably part of what shapes our consciousness. Immanuel Kant said the *a priori* (previous to consciousness) categories of time and space predetermined consciousness, and I'm sure he's right. But no more than does the fact we have hands and fingers instead of fin and wings which shape the way we come in contact with our world and it with us.

    An eagle might have thoughts or sensations which are much more related to and shaped by a beak and claws and wings. Oftentimes the eagle negotiates its relationship to the world through its beak—pecking, tearing, scraping, digging. Very sharp and incisive thoughts. Certainly not thoughts that come from five fingers and two relatively heavy arms and legs. Pointed thoughts. And then the grace of flight.

our humanity. As Chief Joseph said, "...whatever happens to the beasts also happens to the man."

The other night reading late in bed, I discovered I had no pen to mark the passages in the book I needed for future reference. Too tired to get up and look for a pen, I lay there and thought, "There must be some way to mark the places besides a pen." But all I found on my bed stand was a bottle of scented body lotion. Later the next day, I felt a remarkable affinity for my cat friends as I sniffed along the margins of the book I'd been reading the night before, finding my way with my nose to where I'd marked the passages with the scent of the lotion. It made me realize how habituated we are to established modes of consciousness, to the point that we rely on certain senses for certain functions (eyes instead of nose for locating ourselves in time and space), unaware that we have other options. We have come to depend on sight for most of our sensory information, and to negotiate an increasingly visual and abstract world. Cro-Magnon man must have gotten much vital information about, say, the whereabouts of predators or prey, water, fruit through hearing and even smelling, or we might not have evolved through Cro-Magnon lines. Smell, touch, and hearing are all modes of being that we grow more distant from as we leave childhood to make it in a more cerebral and regimented world. That we are losing touch with the senses of smell and hearing is reflected in the paucity of adjectives we have for smells and sounds.

Other animals remind us that there are many uses of the body and senses—even many types of bodies and sensory apparatus, many ways of being in the body and in the physical world, yet our use of our own human bodies gets censored by such a thin veneer of "civilization," socialization and the restrictions of gender roles, not to mention the basic gravity of habit.

Another thing the cat's animality does is to put sexuality in a broader context of sensuality. Balanced out with other sensuous experiences all day long the act of sex becomes just another—perhaps more intense—way to live through the body, and not, as often happens when we are prohibited a sensual relationship to our time and bodies, the only way. In the milieu of our culture, for many men a general sensual deprivation leads to sexual obsession, mostly in the form of fantasy projection about the female body. When he feels so compelled to perform, a man provides himself little time to be happy in his body like the cat; sex becomes the act by which he can at least feel good in his body while satisfying the imperative to act. But even sex for a man is often unconsciously goal-driven, wherein he is more concerned with attaining orgasm and bringing his partner to orgasm, than exploring the vicissitudes of touch.

So the cat brings to the dreamer a more sensuous relationship to time, to his body and senses, to the physical world and all the contingent phenomena that we close ourselves off to when we kill the cat within in order to fit into the performance mode: the bike race, the three piece suit, the factory, the time clock, the success object.

The danger exists for men especially, and for all participants of a masculine or patriarchal culture that prioritizes *productivity* and control over all else, to become dissociated from our bodies and the language of our more subtle and neglected senses. This narrowly focussed purposefulness cuts us off from possibilities of experience and consciousness and the feeling of being connected to nature, and a part of something greater than ourselves.

The dreamer kneeling over the wounded cat is an image suggesting that we need to be less hostile and judgmental toward our wounded selves, more accepting of and nurturing toward our body, its pain, its pleasure, its curiosities, its language…and to become aware how much it is a part of masculine culture, and perhaps American and Western culture and modern technological life in general, to become cut off from our bodies, our physical habitat and time itself by imposing the language of control, or the language of the Industrial Park: efficiency, productivity, profit in such a way that leads to self-denial and precludes deeper connections to self and other.

A Cat Named Rex

About midway through writing this book, one of the last Cat dreams I've had slinked by almost unnoticed—though it occurs to me now to be an especially appropriate place to end this chapter. In the dream, I'm standing in my back yard in the morning sun with a couple male friends. We've taken time away from the nine to five job world and we're just hanging out talking and enjoying the morning sun when a cat named Rex walks up to me. I pick him up and hold him in my arms for a while, scratching his chin and snuggling his head with my face as he purrs, and we're all very content with things at the moment. Then Rex decides he's had enough affection. I set him down and he slinks under the porch to explore. End of dream.

No agonizing imperative to kill him or have him for breakfast this time. In contrast to the Deadline dream, which begins with a competitive race among young men and ends with me symbolically having to kill the cat, this final dream shows that integration of the feline-feminine aspects has replaced my involuntary opposition and hostility to the cat. My obsession with beating the deadline is replaced with enjoying the morning among friends who have, like me, made adequate room for the cat—for Eros and relationship—in our lives.

When I had this dream, a neighbor at the time had a female cat named Rex. In the dream Rex is a male cat. Rex is Latin for "king." As we found in "Happy as a King in a Bean Pod," the king is the symbol of that which integrates and organizes into a coherent kingdom (or self) the various and sometimes conflicting—and in this case previously repressed—aspects and identities of the man. In the dream, my friends and I have left the dogged bike race of the earlier dream and have made time to connect with this animal manifestation of the psyche. The cat has ceased being Other, the external female, and becomes a part of the individual. My friends and I have come to a point in our lives where we've decided we "have the right to decide how to spend the day "(Bly).

7

The Torn Suit
Jealousy in Slow Motion

It is everybody's allotted fate to become conscious of and learn to deal with this shadow…The world will never reach a state of order until this truth is generally recognized…We psychologists have learned, through long and painful experience, that you deprive a man of his best resources when you help him get rid of his complexes. You can only help him become sufficiently aware of them and to start a conscious conflict within himself. In this way the conflict becomes a focus of life. Anything that disappears from your psychological inventory is apt to turn up in the guise of a hostile neighbor, who will inevitably arouse your anger and make you aggressive.

—C.G. Jung (from *The Awakened Warrior*)

The Dream

I'm on an ocean liner in the middle of a long ocean voyage. It is morning and I'm meeting my girlfriend below deck next to the men's room. She's not there when I arrive, so I go in to relieve myself. When I come out into the long hallway she's there talking to a man she knows. They keep talking for what seems a long time without acknowledging me. Though I never wear such formal clothes in waking life, I am wearing a tight button up dress shirt and vest, and holding a suit coat.

I wait and wait, becoming more and more jealous as I watch her talk and laugh animatedly, paying no attention to me. Although only seconds have passed, I storm angrily away through a set of double steel and glass doors which bang shut tightly behind me. It feels good to be running, but I have a feeling I'm getting further from where I need to be. I keep running down a long narrow hallway and through another set of doors that shut hard with an empty iron echo that goes right through me. I run faster down another hallway through a third set of double doors. But this time as I push angrily through the doors, a button on my shirt catches on the door handle and tears the shirt and vest open right above my heart.

I freeze, caught on the door handle, feeling unexpectedly relieved that I've been stopped from running away any further. I look at the tear in the shirt fabric over my heart, and half smile at the poetic justice of being torn open just as I was getting more and more closed off. For a minute I just hang there, gathering myself and feeling a remarkable sense of calm. Then my attention turns to my girlfriend, and I suddenly panic that I'm going to lose her if I don't get back to her. I start running back, desperate to find her, down hallways, through door after door. But the hallways have become like a labyrinth, and I can't find my way back.

*   *   *

Much like in the Mole dream where the dreamer is on his way to his girl-friend's house and the Shaman dream where he's looking for inner connection through connecting with his three-eyes girlfriend, here too it requires a wound-ing or descent—a tearing through the fabric or pattern—to wake the dreamer up to the more conscious relationship he needs to have with himself.

I dreamed this dream the night after dreaming "The Cat's Wound" dream and three months into a new relationship. The night I dreamed this, my girl-friend at the time and I were together at a clothing store, and while I was try-ing on a shirt in the dressing room and about to get her opinion of it, she ran into a man she knew outside my dressing room and divided her attention between him and me—with me becoming jealous.

The dream presents us with a principle, almost antithetical to traditional masculine culture, that when we are able to show or admit to ourselves we are hurt or afraid, we don't need to put so much of our energy (or the national budget) into fear, defensiveness, or blaming others. The dream ego runs away from the infantile self he has always unconsciously handed over to women to take care of. He has to begin a dialogue with this part of himself, relate to it consciously, instead of going through her, and this means giving up the attempt to get others to be responsible for the feelings of abandonment and jealousy that the situation of intimacy brings out in him. He buttons up to hide his hurt and unconsciously blames her for his feelings, but this only gets him more lost.

We become lost to the extent we try to conceal and dissociate ourselves from the sort of feelings we've learned to be ashamed of. The suit I uncharacteristically wear in the dream is associated with the suit the infant's father wears in the King in a Bean Pod dream, and the fraternity boys wear in the Shaman dream—and which have come to symbolize in these dreams a man cut off from the inner life of his feelings. In this case, the feelings are ones I am ashamed to have, especially as a man: dependency, jealousy, and the sense of inadequacy that manifest themselves in my comparing myself with the man my girlfriend is enjoying talking to. *Unable to get to the source of these feelings or beliefs* in myself, *they turn into projections about my girlfriend, questions about her loyalty or desire for me. This is to have regressed to an unconscious infantile identification with another, as the dream ego seems to have done, and as many of us do in romantic love.*

To some extent, my socialization as a man has made it second nature to disown feelings associated with weakness and to compensate with outward demonstrations of control and competency. *In a sense the dream is a parable about the attempt to disown one's shadow self—how it inexorably leads us down labyrinthine hallways and through iron doors of denial and self-alienation into isolation.* If I could *consciously* feel jealous, abandoned and inadequate as I stand next to my girlfriend while she talks to this man, I could, as Jung speaks of above, "start a conscious conflict within" myself. That would help me stay grounded in myself. But, still stuck in the mode of dissociating from these feelings, I immediately switch to anger and blame, fusing with her as I once fused with mother, and run away in order to hurt her, in order to switch the focus onto her. Some of these core feelings and beliefs about ourselves—no matter how false or inaccurate—are so difficult for us to consciously own, we'll use any strategy to avoid consciously feeling these feelings, despite the fact that the instinctive fight or flight response merely preserves our fear unrelated to. Slowing down and becoming aware that these are our projections gradually neutralizes their rule over us. This is when we come to know in the truest sense the meaning of the words from the Talmud, "We do not see things as they are; we see things as we are." When we stop and take our own inventories, we find out about the fears from infancy and childhood that we're still projecting onto others, like projecting a film onto a screen. The film's title might be: *Nightmares I Never Woke From.*

Yet stopping to own our feelings, especially when we're in an intimate relationship with another, can be quite challenging. We like to put the best foot forward. Our fleeing and denial keep us powerless in the face of our most infantile fears and expectations. And of course, the masculine injunction to always appear strong and in control doesn't help us in these matters. We can end up alone, having alienated ourselves not only from the one we love, but from being able to love and tend to ourselves: the dry horror of self-alienation. This is the labyrinth we get lost in when we put on our suits of armor and run away, attempting to dissociate from our weaknesses and wounds. In that vacuum we deny ourselves the relief that comes from owning the wound.

Waiting for her attention to return to him outside the men's room, he monitors her every move looking for signs of the abandonment or betrayal he fears is inevitable, and finally, unable to bear the abandonment he projects is happening, he runs away and abandons her. At this point, the man who has been taught to externalize his emotional life in a relationship to a woman *must become conscious of his projections as projections, especially when we're so focussed on someone else in "love." This is when our unresolved infantile experience of the parents most prefigures our expectations of others in romantic love.* Such a wound we must learn to relate to inwardly. And the dream makes this point rather sharply when it impales the dreamer on the door handle to interrupt his flight from himself.

In *Keeping the Love You Find*, Harville Hendrix observes that when a child doesn't experience reliable warmth and love from his or her parents, he or she gets wounded at the developmental stage of attachment. The lack of sufficient nurture and attention lead to a "clinging" response, brought on by the expectation of scarcity and loss. When the child grows up not trusting attachment, this lack of trust leads to incomplete and difficult separation from the parent(s) and later from a romantic partner. This makes union difficult and separation traumatic.

The situation of intimacy then brings about the expectation of losing it and so he holds on tightly and looks for any evidence of mother or father's imminent departure. Later in life, this expectation can become a painfully self-fulfilling projection. In *Neurosis and Its Treatment*, the psychologist Andrus Angyal characterizes this psychological dynamic as the "fear system" versus the "confidence system," and gives as the quintessential example the infant at mother's breast: when we experience her attention as frequent and reliable, we let go when she pulls away, assuming she'll be back. Or we tire of her attention, and *we* pull away, confidently assuming she'll be there when we're hungry again. But when we experience unreliable nurture, we resist her separateness; when she comes close enough we cling and grab, and worry when she leaves that she'll never come back. Of course, at that time in our lives we are totally dependent on the parents for our survival, so mother or father's not coming back would literally mean our death.

We can see what a difficult situation the dream ego is in (and men and now women in general) when he feels wounded yet has learned to deny woundedness as shameful, weak, and unproductive. The rejection of our primary feelings leads us out of a mindful relationship to ourselves, out of our bodies and into this ungrounded, untrustworthy air of projection and dependency where we regress to the fight or flight primordial brain. The whole basis of humanity is the interruption of these automatic responses by making room for awareness. To be able to make room for awareness we need to be beside ourselves, observing, detached as much as possible from our ego, and this, my friend, requires the tremendous step of accepting ourselves as we are. Then we have choices. Otherwise we remain trapped in our reactions to others.

The dream makes sure that his running "away" at least leads him to the self he needs to confront. The door handle catches him in his self-alienated flight and wounds him into the attentiveness he needs to be showing himself, especially in the face of all his projections about his lover.

The flip side of having for centuries designated men to be the protectors and aggressors is that it has become almost instinctive for many men to get angry and defensive rather than let themselves feel threatened, vulnerable or hurt. The fight or flight reaction has become so automatic that it is possible to have no awareness of it, and a man's healing will depend on slowing down this whole process so he can become aware of the feelings he has unconsciously made someone else responsible for. Otherwise this dissociation from his own shadow side can lead to desperate and tragic actions. Robert Hopcke's remarks about treating his male clients are worth repeating, "I often find myself devoting the better part of the first year of therapy with a male patient simply to the development of a workable emotional awareness." As the dream suggests, this emotional awareness becomes even more important the closer we get to someone else. In other words, the more intimate we get with someone else, the more prone we are to losing a conscious relationship to ourselves, especially where we are wounded.

Appropriately, it is only when the dream ego is stopped from running away any further by his shirt and vest catching on the door handle that he feels any peace of mind or centeredness; he is caught in the act and forced to relate to his inner self. Sometimes it is only when we lose a lover that we are brought to this confrontation with the deeper self.

Love

What inevitably happens in love—if we have set out to get someone to take responsibility for our shadow—is that we get handed back the self we set out to avoid. When we get close to someone they inevitably engage our deepest intimacy fears and needs left over from infancy, thereby giving us the opportunity to reclaim our wounded selves, presenting us with the terms of our earliest self-alienation, and thus of our wholeness and authenticity.

Ultimately, any relationship hands this back to us. *Because when our partner or lover ceases to be a fantasy projection, we feel again our separateness.* And this means we feel our wounds. If lovers make this process a conscious part of their relationship, it can be the very thing that helps each become whole again, reconciled with their abandoned selves. Otherwise, we tend to get co-dependently enmeshed where we are unconsciously wounded.

In *Keeping the Love You Find*, Harville Hendrix maintains that "the unconscious mission of all couples" is for each partner to heal the wounds of childhood (147). This means the wounds must first be opened up, and many couples don't stay together when the wounds or moles show up

As in the Cat's Wound dream, this innermost wounded self is gotten to only through relationship with others. We unconsciously seek to replicate our original experience of intimacy—no matter how painful or dysfunctional—because that early experience is what triggers our unconscious infantile hunger for attachment. It is only through replaying it that we can consciously recover the more authentic self we censored or repressed in infancy. According to Hendrix, romantic love is "nature's anesthetic" which blinds us to the fact that the person we are most passionately attracted to is one who will replicate the pattern by which we were first "disappointed" in love by the parent(s) (72). To replicate this situation, only this time consciously, is where our healing will happen.

In love, we are usually not "powerfully" attracted to someone who doesn't engage our wounds. The power of the attraction is based on how the chemistry with another feels like our earliest and most intense attachment to the parents. However, when we are consciously taking care of our psychic wounds, we begin to grow out of the unconscious patterns of childhood into a true choice in the matter of a love partner. Many of our relationships succeed only in helping us to discover that the people we choose are part of the repetition of a pattern we began in infancy with the parents where we were wounded at the attachment stage. Here we are most unconscious because the strategies in infancy to deal with trauma involve stopping awareness of pain, shutting out or altering bad or scary thoughts, again, what Stephen Wolinsky in *The Dark Side of the Inner Child* calls a "trance state." "When the observer fuses with the inner child resources that could be used feel unavailable" (20). Where these places are most unconscious in ourselves is where we attach most passionately to others. The intoxication we sometimes feel in the early stages of romantic love blurs the reality that this intimate situation is about to engage our deepest wounds, the healing of which serves a much deeper purpose than merely gratifying our ego needs.

Hence, the eventual failure of the "merger" with our partner is the beginning of the far more important work of a conscious relationship together, predicated on each partner continuing to relate consciously to the wounds and anxieties that intimacy triggers. It seems all too clear that if we can't be on intimate terms with ourselves, we'll have difficulty being on intimate terms with someone else. Sooner or later, we are left to deal with the relationship we have to ourselves. Love requires of us the ability to surrender our ego needs to the greater ideal of union with another; this first necessitates that we can surrender our ego defenses to a greater awareness of self.

While the cat in "The Cat's Wound" dream teaches the man that kneeling beside his wounds and opening them up are the first steps to healing, "The Torn Suit" dream shows how easily we lose this relationship with ourselves and revert back to defensiveness once a lover enters the picture. The relationship pierces our armor, as it pierces the dream ego, tearing open our desired public image and exposing the deeper self, along with its wounds. In psychological parlance, the relationship "relativizes" the ego.

The labyrinth of hallways is the perfect metaphor for what happens to us psychologically when we deny our wounds or try to make someone else responsible for them. When he closes off to his wound and focuses on her, he leaves his body and loses this grounding in himself, and enters the dangerous rarefied air of his own unconscious, fearful projections—the time we are most likely to wound others. Which is why he feels such an unexpected relief when the door handle catches one of his buttons and tears open his shirt and vest.

The symbolism here couldn't be more to the point: he gets caught by the instruments of his denial—the buttons and button up dress shirt and vest which symbolize concealing the body and the body of "undesirable" feelings in order to keep up the appearance of success, invulnerability and control, and the door and door handle, by which he attempts to shut out his jealousy and the infantile fears he feels so ashamed to be associated with. If he can begin to observe these feelings, he can start to grow out of this unconscious infantile identification with his girlfriend. But the big backdrop to this problem concerns how our society regularly shames men from accepting what then become unacceptable weaknesses. Denied, they simply grow worse.

The real terror of jealousy, rage and fear is that in our attempt not to feel them, we lose a conscious relationship to ourselves, and experience not the fear, not the abandonment, not the jealousy, but only the panic of fleeing ourselves. The dream intervenes to tell the dreamer that he can't get through the door with this false image of himself on this voyage of intimacy. As he hangs by his torn shirt caught on the door handle, he feels the relief of the fugitive who has just been caught and, by being caught, is saved from a lonely life of aliases and disguises on the run. Thus he is relieved of maintaining images and facades of success. This is when we, ironically, fail into our own depths. The wound forces him to relate to himself directly, instead of, as in infancy, having this security mediated through another. Of course, it is invaluable to have a good therapist or counselor to help us understand and become responsible for our wounds. This is when we transform our wounds into greater capacity for life.

It is tempting to read the dreamer's focus on his girlfriend as the sort of imbalanced dependence on the female that the absence of adequate fathering reinforces—and while I think this goes far to explain the crisis in the dream and in many men's lives, it's not the whole story. No amount of fathering (or mothering) or cultural initiation gives us our center, our inner self: this requires conscious work, and the situation of intimacy—emotional, sexual, psychological—almost always creates tension and uncertainty along the borders of the self. But we do find again and again, the absence of reliable and adequate guidance from the parents and culture maroons us in the dependencies and isolation of childhood.

More specifically, the idea here is that young men need help leaving (or balancing) their dependencies on mother. When the father or cultural fathers aren't available, the sons take this unresolved dependency to their lovers, where it is increasingly difficult to identify, much less transform. The struggle with unresolved infantile dependencies can lead to the agonized dance between iron man denial and infantile enmeshment, controlling of his partner, emotional hostage-taking, or flight from relationships that bring about the conflict. Young men, and men of all ages, really, need help negotiating this psychological terrain. It needs to be contextualized by a capable guide, or the struggle can lead to shame, isolation, depression and rage.

In the dream, the tear in the dream ego's vest and shirt interrupt his focus on his girlfriend for his well-being, and he is momentarily relieved of the terror of being externalized. Now he can trace his fear of abandonment and feelings of jealousy and possessiveness to something he can relate to *"in himself"* and eventually transform the fears. Taking responsibility for ourselves is a great relief, as if we've been falling out of control, or pulled helplessly out to sea, and our feet suddenly touch bottom and we finally have a foothold. It is the one moment in the dream that he feels at peace, centered, whole unto himself. Guy Corneau describes this moment, "When an individual stops telling himself it's someone else's fault, a new world opens up for him…The road to responsibility is the road to freedom…"(*Absent Fathers* 168).

He hangs there impaled on the door handle feeling—paradoxically—calm and centered. But as soon as his focus shifts from his wound back to his lover's whereabouts, and he sets out to find her, he panics and the hallways become labyrinths along which he races, getting further and further from that brief moment of security. As in the dream, the focus on others for our sense of self effectively transforms our world into a labyrinth of hallways we get lost and powerless in. Impaled on the door handle, the dreamer surrenders to an awareness of himself and is freed from the labyrinthine nightmare of trying to control people, lovers, situations. This surrender to awareness opens us up to our own profound inner resources that we lost access to when we covered up our wounds.

APPENDIX

Masculinity and Feminism

As I mentioned earlier, I am interested in what our culture has tended to alienate men from on an inner level while asking them to perform the traditional roles of provider, protector, and producer. Since feminism has for the last thirty years been the dominant critique of male as well as female roles in our society, a few words are in order regarding feminism.

Feminism and women's studies programs in colleges across the country have asked how "patriarchal" culture has alienated women from their "power," their wholeness as individuals. This has helped to free women from alienating stereotypes, expectations, sex and social roles, and in many ways helped to free men as well. But to the extent feminism has equated a woman's experience of powerlessness with male power, it misunderstands men (and male alienation), often while blaming them. In its just concern for how our society has alienated women from themselves and excluded them from a voice or social power, feminists have tended to emphasize and exaggerate the dark side of men and masculinity, while emphasizing female suffering and victimization, and mythologizing female sensitivity and "superior" capacity for love and nurture. It has largely ignored the dark side of women and positive images of men and masculinity. This latter shortcoming impoverishes both men's and women's imagination and ability to reach toward any ideal of masculinity, and thus toward any ideal of union between men and women. (One can't idealize women while demonizing men and still have enough left over for the possibility of love.)

Some feminists have developed a language—a shorthand—laden with assumptions, generalizations and judgments which are inordinately easy to impose on *all* men. This has negatively colored our collective image of men and masculinity, so that even his strength, his wildness and desire can easily be devalued as mere "machismo," "chauvinism," "sexism," or adolescence. His hard work, dedication to the family, his agony and creative genius, his poetry and suffering get knocked as "patriarchal privilege," "old boys network" advantage. His sexual desire is both titillated and shamed by the same women, and until recently there has been little room in feminist thought for his suffering despite the fact that men continue to die 10% sooner than women, commit suicide and succumb to drug and alcohol addiction at four times the rate of women, and take on 95% of the hazardous jobs in the country while suffering 95% of the injuries—including dying in wars (*The Myth of Male Power*). And on top of this, when one factors in expenses (child support, alimony) the average net income for male heads of households in the United States is actually less than for female heads of households. Yet the popular notion is that "men have all the power." [1]

The preceding dreams test this assumption. The ready-made nomenclature established by feminism for interpreting men's motives and behavior is too often based on a woman's experience of powerlessness and victimization. This is not to devalue a woman's suffering or to dismiss the need to transform social roles and attitudes that curtail a woman's self-expression; it is a necessary corrective to a perspective that, when unbalanced, is capable of causing more harm than good, more fear than hope, more blame than understanding. We can't go on trying to heal girls and women without trying to understand how boys and men are wounded.

Meanwhile, men have no such ready-made nomenclature or social shorthand to describe—let alone validate—how they feel victimized by the social roles they are nonetheless expected to fulfill, or to describe their experience of the dark side of the mother and women as abusive, heartless and insensitive to his needs and his experience—; he has no language for this despite the fact that female to male violence is roughly equal to male to female violence, both between couples and from parents to children.[2]

---

1.   Farrell in *The Myth of Male Power*, and Andrew Kimbrell in *The Masculine Mystique: The Politics of Masculinity* both citing figures from the Bureau of the Census.
2.   *Myth of Male Power* 214-228; *Why Men Are The Way They Are* 227-231. These figures are also based on statistics from the Bureau of the Census, and also reported in Andrew Kimbrell's *The Masculine Mystique*.

My aim here is not to win bragging rights for victimhood, but to show that we as a culture—in part because of thirty years of feminist dominated gender theory—are sorely lacking a language and conceptual framework for understanding men's experience of powerlessness, fear, needs and love. Without this, sons can't leave childhood, and men can never grow up. This cultural climate, coupled with an absent or unavailable father, makes it all the easier for a young man to accept definitions of himself that are oblivious and hostile to his experience of love, desire, creativity, grief, needs, powerlessness, fear and isolation—definitions of himself and other men that are oblivious to his humanity. Thus denied a language for his innermost feelings, he becomes doubly alienated from and hostile to these places in himself. It takes both men and women, fathers and mothers, to give a son belief in his own humanity. Any perspective or attitude which denies him that, helps to create rather than heal the monsters we most fear and loathe.

Feminism has made both possible and necessary a similar critique of male socialization. This work is of great urgency since our socialization is by and large failing to help young men and women move from childhood to adulthood. One need only check out the statistics of gang violence to find out how fatherless sons are faring in our country. In what has been perhaps the most victimized sector of our population, murder is the leading cause of death for black males between the ages of fourteen and twenty four (*Myth of Male Power*).

The problem with masculinity (as with femininity) is in the ways it alienates us from our wholeness as human beings. Both men and women become alienated from significant parts of themselves in their socialization along gender lines. As the psychologist Harville Hendrix succinctly puts it, men still get rewarded for being "stoic and assertive," and women for being "helpful and cute" (*Keeping the Love You Find*). Farrell sees traditional gender roles as still emphasizing women as the "sex object," and men as the "success object" (*Why Men are the Way They Are*). Others have pointed out that women are allowed tears and men are allowed anger (Sam Keen, *Fire in the Belly*). Still others maintain that one's childhood experience in the family plays a greater part than gender socialization. Whatever the imbalances, it falls on us as individuals to reckon with them.

Those fortunate enough find the proper balance or guidance, or a good therapist, perhaps, who enacts the initiatory rituals the shaman has stewarded for centuries and which have in our tribe grown cold and blown away like the ashes of a sachem's ceremonial fire. Initiation in our tribe has become largely a matter of economics and survival, which means there isn't much of it happening on a psychological or spiritual level—except what happens in organized religion, and that can bring its own dysfunction as well. Consequently, more pressure is put on the family to provide this guidance. And yet, the extended family of uncles and aunts, grandparents, grandchildren, nieces, and nephews that brought old and young together and gave children a variety of mentors, is increasingly a rarity. And to make matters worse, in the majority of homes both parents are working and have less time than ever for their children, who become, as in the first dream, marooned on paths that don't lead us out of our childhood dependencies and traumas.

To trace where most of us have become self-alienated leads us back to our experience of our parents whose behavior has also been shaped by social expectations, social and gender roles. For a man, his self-alienation often leads back to his experience of his father as emotionally unavailable or unreliable. The mother-son relationship is no less important, but my angle on masculine consciousness and its relationship to intimacy with women begins with his experience of his father and the cultural fathers as absent. This is not the case for all men; it is the case for many men, and possibly most men, perhaps without them even being conscious of it, since the lack of awareness of one's wounds is central to the condition of consciousness explored throughout this book in my attempt to help come up with a language for understanding, rather than for blaming.

Bibliography

Angyal, Andrus. *Neurosis and Its Treatment: A Holistic Theory*. New York: The Viking Press, circa 1980. (Unpublished revised ms. from ed. Richard Jones.)

Bly, Robert. *Iron John: A Book About Men*. Reading, MA: Addison-Wesley Publishing Company, Inc., 1990.

——. "A World of Half Adults," in *The Utne Reader*, _____

——. "What Men Really Want," in Rick Fields, ed. *Challenge of the Heart*: Boston, Shambhala, 1985.

Barrie, J.M. *Peter Pan, or The Boy Who Would Not Grow Up*. New York: Charles Scribner's Sons, 1928.

Barthes, Roland. *Mythologies*. Trans. Annette Lavers. New York: Hill and Wang, 1986.

Campbell, Joseph. *The Hero With a Thousand Faces*, Princeton NJ: Princeton University Press, 2nd ed. 1968.

——, comentary by. *The Complete Grimm's Fairy Tales*, New York: Pantheon Books, 1974.

——, with Bill Moyers. The Power of Myth, New York: Doubleday, 1988.

Clatterbaugh, Kenneth. *Contemporary Perspectives on Masculinity*,

Conrad, Joseph. Heart of Darkness.

——. Lord Jim.

Corneau, Guy. *Absent Fathers, Lost Sons: The Search for Masculine Identity*, Boston: Shambhala, 1991.

Daigle, Richard J. *The Mentor Dictionary of Mythology and the Bible*, New York: New American Library, 1973.

Dante, Alighieri., *The Divine Comedy: 1: Inferno*, Trans. John Sinclair. New York: Oxford University Press, 1982.

Dickinson, Emily. *The Complete Poems of Emily Dickinson*. Boston: Little Brown & Company, 1960.

Dijkstra, Bram. *Idols of Perversity: Fantasies of Feminine Evil in Fin-de-Siecle Culture*. New York: Oxford University Press, 1986.

Dreiser, Theodore. *The Financier*. New York: New American Library, 1981.

———. Sister Carrie.

Eliot, T.S. *Collected Poems: 1909-1962*. San Diego: Harcourt Brace Javonovich, 1970.

Encyclopedia Americana. Danbury, Conn.: Grolier, 1995.

Erikson, Erik H. *Insight and Responsibility: Lectures on the Ethical Implications of Psychoanalytic Insight*. New York: W.W. Norton, 1964.

Farrell, Warren, Ph.D. *The Myth of Male Power: Why Men are the Disposable Sex*, New York: Simon & Schuster, 1993.

Farrell, Warren, Ph.D. *Why Men Are the Way They Are: The Male-Female Dynamic*, New York: McGraw-Hill Book Co., 1986.

Faulkner, William. *The Sound and the Fury*. New York: Vintage, 1954.

Fields, Rick, ed., *The Awakened Warrior*,

Fitzgerald, F. Scott. *The Great Gatsby*. New York: Charles Scribner's Sons, 1925.

———. *Tender is the Night*. New York: Bantam, 1951 c1934.

Franz, Marie-Louise von. *Puer Aeturnus: A Psychological Study of the Adult Struggle with the Paradise of Childhood.* Sigo Press, 1981.

Freud, Sigmund, *Beyond the Pleasure Principle.* Trans.James Strachey. New York: W.W. Norton, 1961.

——. *Civilization and Its Discontents,* Trans. James Strachey. New York: W.W. Norton, 1961.

——. *The Ego and the Id.* Trans.Joan Riviere. New York: W.W. Norton, 1962.

——. *The Interpretation of Dreams.* Trans. James Strachey. New York: Avon Books, 1972.

——. *Jokes and Their Relation to the Unconscious.* Trans. James Strachey New York: W.W. Norton, 1963.

——. *Three Case Histories,* New York: Collier Books, 1977.

——. *Three Essays on the Theory of Sexuality.* Trans. James Strachey. New York: Harper, 1962.

Gerzon, Mark. *A Choice of Heroes: The Changing Face of American Manhood.* Boston: Houghton Mifflin, 1982.

Goethe, Johann Wolfgang. *Faust/Part One.* Trans. Philip Wayne. Middlesex: Penguin Books, Ltd, 1982.

——. *Faust/Part Two.* Trans. Philip Wayne. Middlesex; Penguin Books, Ltd, 1982.

Goldberg, Herb, *The Hazards of Being Male: Surviving the Myth of Masculine Priviledge. New York: Nash Pub., 1976.*

——. *The New Male: From Self-Destruction to Self-Care.* New York: New American Library, 1980.

Golding, William. *Lord of the Flies.* New York: Coward-McCann, 1962.

Gurian, Michael. *Mothers, Sons and Lovers.* Boston: Shambhala, 1994.

——. *The Prince and the King*,

Hamilton, Edith. *Mythology*. New York: The New American Library, 1942.

Hartsock, Nancy C.M. *Money, Sex and Power: Toward a Feminist Historical Materialism*. Boston: Northeastern University Press, 1983.

Hauberlin, Hermann, & Emma Gunther. *The Indians of Puget Sound*. Seattle: University of Washington Press, 1930.

Hemingway, Ernest. *A Farewell to Arms*. New York: Charles Scribner's Sons, 1929.

——. *For Whom the Bell Tolls*. New York: Scribner's, 1968.

——. *The Old Man and the Sea*. New York: Charles Scribner's Sons, 1952.

——. *The Sun Also Rises*. New York: Charles Scribner's Sons, 1954.

——. *"The Short Happy Life of Francis Macomber"*

Hendrix, Harville, Ph.D. *Keeping the Love You Find*. New York: Pocket Books, 1992.

Hillman, James. *The Dream and the Underworld*. New York: Harper & Row, Publishers, 1973.

Hollis, James. *Under Saturn's Shadow: The Wounding and Healing of Men*. Toronto: Inner City Books, 1994.

Hopcke, Robert. *Men's Dreams, Men's Healing: A Psychotherapist Explores a New View of Masculinty Through Jungian Dreamwork*. Boston: Shambhala, 1990.

Johnson, Robert. *He: Understanding Masculine Psychology*. New York: Perennial Library/Harper &Row Publishers, 1989.

——. *Transformation: Understanding the Three Levels of Masculine Consciousness*. San Francisco: *HarperSanFrancisco*, 1991.

———. *We: Understanding the Psychology of Romantic Love*. San Francisco: Harper & Row Publishers, 1983.

Jones, Ernest. *The Life and Work of Sigmund Freud*. Middlesex: Penguin Books, 1977.

Jones, Richard M., *The Dream Poet*

Jung, Carl Gustav. *C.G. Jung Speaking: Interviews and Encounters*. London; Picador Books, 1980.

———. *Dreams*. Princeton NJ: Princeton University Press,1974.

———. *Memories, Dreams, Reflections*. Ed. Anelia Jaffe. New York:Vintage Books, 1965.

———. *Modern Man in Search of a Soul*. Trans. W.S. Dell & Carry E. Baynes. San Diego: Harcourt Brace Javonovich, 1933.

———. *Psychology and Religion*. New Haven:Yale University Press, 1938.

———. *Word and Image*. Ed. Anelia Jaffe. Princeton: Princeton University Press, 1979.

Katsanzakis, Nikos. *Zorba the Greek*. New York: Touchstone,1952.

Keen, Sam. *Fire in the Belly: On Being a Man*. New York: Bantam Books, 1991.

Kierkegaard, Soren. *Fear and Trembling, and the Sickness Unto Death*. Trans. Walter Lowrie. Garden City, N.Y.: Doubleday, 1954.

Keyes, Paul. *Zen Bone, Zen Flesh: A Collection of Zen and Pre-Zen Writings*. New York: Anchor, 1989.

Kimbrell, Andrew. *The Masculine Mystique*. New York: Ballantine, 1995.

Kipnis, Aaaron R., Ph.D. *Knights Without Armor: A Practical Guide for Men in Quest of Masculine Soul*. New York: A Jeremy Tarcher/Putnam Book, 1991.

Kundera, Milan. *The Book of Laughter and Forgetting*. Trans. Michael Henry Heime. New York: Knopf, 1980.

——. *The Farewell Party*. Trans. Peter Kussi. New York: Knopf, 1976.

——. *The Joke*. New York: HarperCollins,1992.

——. *Life is Elsewhere*. Trans. Peter Kussi. New York: Knopf, 1974.

——. *The Unbearable Lightness of Being*. Trans. Michael Henry Heime. New York: Harper and Row, 1984.

Lawrence, D. H. *Women in Love*. Middlesex: Penguin, 1982.

Lee, John. *The Flying Boy: Healing the Wounded Man*. Deer Beach, FL: Health Communications, Inc., 1989.

Leonard, Linda Schierse. *The Wounded Woman: Healing the Father-Daughter Relationship*. Boston: Shambhala, 1982.

Lukacs, George. *The Meaning of Contemporay Realism*. Trans. John and Necke Mander. London: Merlin Press, 1963.

Melville, Herman. *Moby Dick, or The Whale*. New York: The Modern Library, 1982.

Mitchell, Steven. *Tao Te Ching*. New York: HarperPerennial, 1988.

Miller, Alice. *The Drama of the Gifted Child*. New York: Basic Books, 1981.

Moore, Robert, & Douglas Gillette. *King, Warrior, Magician, Lover: Rediscovering the Archetypes of the Mature Masculine*. San Francisco: HarperSanFrancisco, 1990.

——. *The Magician Within: Accessing the Shaman in the Male Psyche*. New York: William Morrow & Co, 1993.

Moore, Thomas. *Care of the Soul*. New York: HarperCollinsPublishers, 1992.

Neihardt, John G. *Black Elk Speaks: Being the Life Story of a Holy Man of the Oglala Sioux*. Lincoln, Nebraska: University of Nebraska Press,1979.

Nietzsche, Friederick. *The Birth of Tragedy and the Case of Wagner.* Trans. Walter Kaufmann. New York: Bantam, 1967.

——. *On the Genealogy of Morals.* Trans. Walter Kaufmann. New York: Vintage Books, 1967.

Rich, Adrienne. *On Lies, Secrets, and Silence*: Selected Prose, 1966-1978. New York: Norton, 1979.

Rilke, Ranier Maria. *Duino Elegies.* Boston: Shambhala, 1992.

Rumi, Jelaluddin. *Open Secret: Versions of Rumi.* Trans. John Moyne & Coleman Barks. Putney, Vt, Threshold Books, 1984.

Sattel, Jack. "The Inexpressive Male: Tragedy or Sexual Politics?"

Schwenger, Peter. *Phallic Critiques: Masculinity and Twentieth Century Literature.* London; Boston: Routledge and Kegan Paul, 1984.

Shakespeare, William. *The Complete Works of William Shakespeare.* New York: Doubleday, 1936.

——. *The Riverside Shakespeare.* Boston: Houghton Mifflin, 1974.

Star Wars: Episode IV: A New Hope. Dir. George Lucas. Perf. Mark Hamill, Harrison Ford, Carrie Fisher, Peter Cushing, Alec Guiness, Anthony Daniels, Kenny Baker, voice of James Earl Jones (as Darth Vader). Panavision, 1977.

——. *Episode V: The Empire Strikes Back.* Dir. Irvin Kershner. Perf. Mark Hamill, Harrison Ford, Carrie Fisher, Billy Dee Williams, Anthony Daniels, David Prowse, Peter Mayhew, Kenny Baker, Frank Oz, Clive Revill, Julian Glover, John Ratzenberger, voice of James Earl Jones (as Darth Vader). Panavision, 1980.

——. *Episode VI: Return of the Jedi.* Dir. Richard Marquand. Perf. Mark Hamill, Harrison Ford, Carrie Fisher, Billy Dee Williams, Anthony Daniels, Peter Mayhew, Sebastian Shaw, Ian McDiamid, David Prowse, Alec Guiness, Kenny Baker, Denis Lawson, Warwick Davis, voices of James Earl Jones (as Darth Vader) and Frank Oz. Panavision, 1983.

Stoker, Bram. *Dracula*. New York: Amereon House, 1981 c 1897.

Stoltenberg, Robert, *Refusing to be a Man: Essays on Sex and Justice*, Portland, OR: Breidenbush Books, 1989.

The Swimmer. Dir. Frank Perry. Perf. Burt Lancaster, Janet Landgard, Janice Rule, Tony Bickley, Marge Champion, Bill Fiore, Kim Hunter, Joan Rivers. From John Cheever short story. 1968.

Theweleit, Klaus. *Male Fantasies, Volume 1: Women, Floods, Bodies, History*. Minneapolis: University of Minnesota Press, 1987.

———. *Male Fantasies Volume 2: Male Bodies: Psychoanalyzing the White Terror*. Minneapolis: University of Minnesota Press, 1989.

Thomas, Dylan. *Collected Poems: The Collected Poems of Dylan Thomas 1934-1952*. New York: New Directions Books, 1971.

Thoreau, Henry David. *Walden and Civil Disobedience*. Ed. Owen Thomas. New York: W.W. Norton & Co., 1966.

Trachtenberg, Allen. *The Incorporation of America: Culture and Society in the Gilded Age*. New York: Hill and Wang, 1982.

Tripp, Edward. *Crowell's Handbook of Classical Mythology*. New York: Thomas Crowell Publishers, 1970.

Trungpa, Chogyam. *Meditation in Action*. Boston: Shambhala, 1991.

Turner, Frederick W. *The Portable North American Indian Reader*. New York: Penguin Books, 1974.

Whitman, Walt. *Walt Whitman: Complete Poetry and Collected Prose*. New York: The Library of America, 1982.

Williams, Raymond. *Marxism and Literature*. New York: Oxford, 1977.

Wolinsky, Steven. *The Dark Side of the Inner Child.* Connecticut: Bramble Books, 1993.

Woolf, Virginia. *Mrs. Dalloway.* New York: Harcourt Brace & World, c 1925.

———. *To the Lighthouse.* New York: Harcourt Brace, 1927.

———. *The Waves.* San Diego: Harcourt Brace, 1931.

Zukav, Gary. *Seat of the Soul.* New York: Fireside, 1990.

Others:

"Silence of the Frogs," article New York Times Magazine, 12-13-92

978-0-595-40189-5
0-595-40189-9

Printed in Poland
by Amazon Fulfillment
Poland Sp. z o.o., Wrocław